THE LIVING WILDERNESS

Atholl Deer Forests

THE LIVING WILDERNESS

Atholl Deer Forests

by
John Kerr

Foreword by His Grace the Duke of Atholl

Publisher
Jamieson & Munro

To Patricia with love

ISBN
1 900489 02 3

Published by
Jamieson & Munro, 38 Tay Street, Perth PH1 5TT

Photography by
John Kerr

Front Cover Design
"Sronphadruig" by Roger Lee, Calvine

Printed by
SUNPRINT, 38 Tay Street. Perth PH1 5TT.

CONTENTS

THE ATHOLL LANDSCAPE

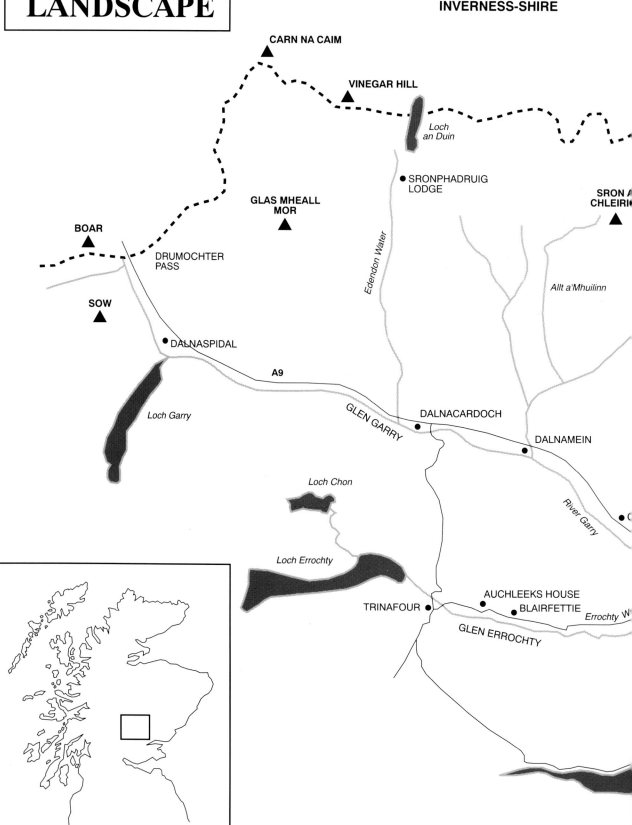

INVERNESS-SHIRE

MINIG.

CARN NA CAIM

VINEGAR HILL

Loch an Duin

SRONPHADRUIG LODGE

SRON A CHLEIRIC

GLAS MHEALL MOR

BOAR

Edendon Water

Allt a'Mhuilinn

DRUMOCHTER PASS

SOW

DALNASPIDAL

A9

Loch Garry

GLEN GARRY

DALNACARDOCH

DALNAMEIN

Loch Chon

River Garry

Loch Errochty

AUCHLEEKS HOUSE

TRINAFOUR

BLAIRFETTIE

Errochty W

GLEN ERROCHTY

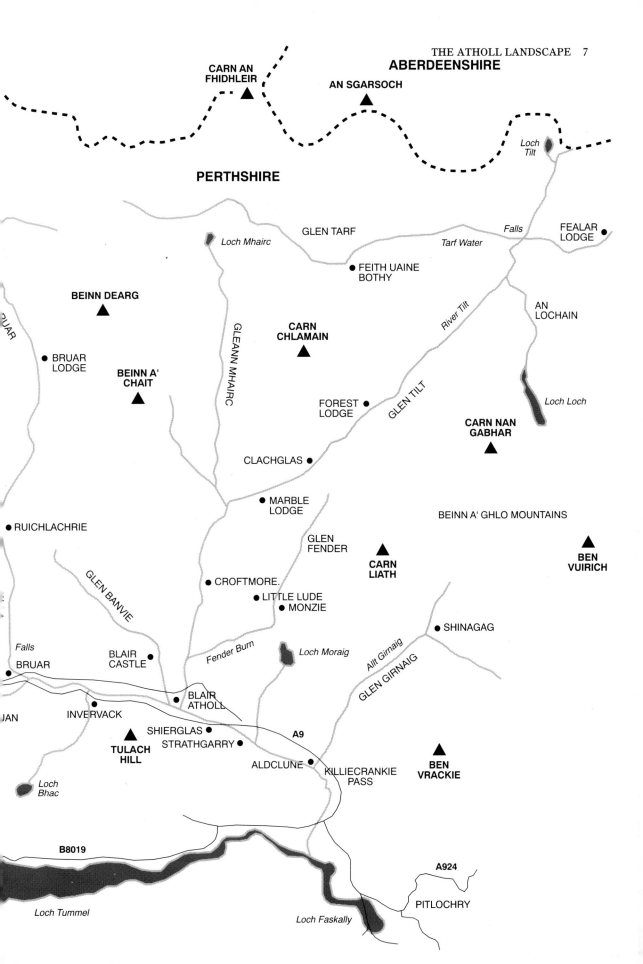

FOREWORD

His Grace the Duke of Atholl

His Grace the Duke of Atholl, outside Blair Castle.

It is not everyone who is asked to write an introduction to a book about his own estate. Well, this has happened to me and it has been most interesting, reading John Kerr's views, knowing both him and the estate well. He does not, for instance, omit parts which have been sold, such as Dalnaspidal and Dalnacardoch, disposed of in 1942 and 1943 respectively. Other parts sold were Fealar in 1935, Glenfernate in 1927 and Loch Valigan in 1948. Fealar and Glenfernate I felt little sorrow about but Loch Valigan seemed to be becoming more and more a ridiculous expense and it is much better that it should be run by Lude.

Nowadays we are being attacked for having too many deer on our ground and we are encouraged to shoot as many as possible in the season. So far I have resisted stoutly and it is not my intention to do this now or in the future. However we have increased our numbers and it seems to me that these are now perfectly adequate for the area which they cover.

My predecessor, the 8th Duke, wrote an introduction to a previous work, published in the 1920s, called "Deer Stalking in Scotland" by Alex McConnachie, in which he said many things, some of which still apply. He concluded with a translation of the deerstalkers' Gaelic toast:

The day we see you, the day we don't;
The day we kill a deer, the day we won't;
We wish you well.

Blair Castle

INTRODUCTION

Dictionary definitions of the word "wilderness" describe it as "wild or uncultivated land" and " a pathless or desolate tract of any kind". The origin of the word is particularly relevant in this instance, as it means a "wild deer promontory".

The deer forests of Atholl cover an area of several hundred square miles of inhospitable mountainous terrain north of the Pass of Killiecrankie in Perthshire. Two hundred years ago, and more, the glens which make up large parts of these deer forests were populated by hundreds of people living and working out their lives in what are now now largely deserted places.

The Statistical Account of 1792 for the parish, written by the Rev. James MacLagan, stated under the heading "Game" that:

> In an extensive forest, and over many other parts of the hills, there are a great number of red deer; in and near the woods, there are roe-deer, almost every where there are plenty of hares, and, on the high mountains, white hares, which in summer, have bluish spots. In the hills and woods are foxes, wild cats, pole cats, martins, weasels, and shrew mice: In the waters, otters. We have also two species of the badger. Of the winged kind, there are, on the tops of the mountains, ptarmagans; in the hills, grouse; near the woods, black game, and partridges below. The ravenous birds are, eagles, buzzards, hawks of various kinds, ravens, carion crows, and magpies. The migratory birds are similar to those usual in the Highlands.

Attempts were made to grow crops right up to the 1,400 feet level, while cattle, horses, goats and a few sheep grazed in the lush pastures of the summer shielings at the heads of these glens. By the end of the eighteenth century problems of existence in these upland glens were intensifying. By continuing old, out-dated farming practices the value of the soil was decreasing and with a growing number of people trying to eke out a living, with their increased numbers of livestock, severe degeneration of already poor land was further aggravated. Life for many had become one of bare subsistence, with the Rev. John Stewart, the Blair Atholl minister commenting that "their principal aliment was animal food".

Added to this, the powers of the landowners were absolute, with the power to move and evict tenants who displeased them or got in the way of their improvements. The tenants with their straying livestock on the summer shielings were regarded by the landowners as nuisances who either scared off or poached their deer. They did not hold to the belief of the Highlander that he had a right to "a salmon from the river, a tree from the forest and a deer from the mountain". The forests and their bounds were patrolled and protected by gamekeepers. Some, like John Crerar, were men of vision. He was the longest serving of them all and developed a special relationship with the Dukes he served, writing regular reports about everything he saw and heard in the course of his work. Many extracts of his reports and those by the estate factors and other gamekeepers appear throughout the book, showing the interplay between tenants, keepers and lairds, adding a contemporary feel through their first hand eye-witness accounts.

A change of emphasis from the old methods of paying rent in kind and through labour to a money-based rental for cash-hungry lairds was a contributory factor to leases expiring. Added to this, the introduction of sheep, which at once meant fewer farms with troublesome tenants, seemed to promise more lucrative financial returns for the landowners, as well as freeing up the old shieling grounds for the return of deer. However, the sheep in their turn brought their own problems. Cattle at best are general grazers, keeping down the coarser grasses, whereas sheep nibble only at the finer, lusher pasture. Thus the vegetation deteriorated allowing heather and bracken to spread.

In the early 1800s landowners saw the growing financial potential of leasing their deer forests and lodges to a new class of wealthy shooting tenants and slowly but surely even the shepherds were replaced by sportsmen. This fashionable influx of seasonal visitors grew dramatically until the middle of the nineteenth century when it was called "the English invasion". By 1900 the glens were virtually empty of farming tenants and the Tullibardine Commission which had been set up to investigate the amount of land set aside for shooting purposes, concluded in 1909 that: "The Atholl Deer Forest is of such a barren soil that it is totally unsuitable for small holdings, allotments, pendicles or crofts".

In-depth research of these forests has revealed much information about their formation and management. There are many pictures of various aspects of hunting in Victorian times and portraits in words and pictures of the gamekeepers of the nineteenth century will help the reader to turn back the clock over 150 years and get a feel for life as it was then, while the present day reports bring us right up to date.

John Kerr, Old Struan

This is a wild land, country of my choice,
With harsh craggy mountain, moor ample and bare.
Seldom in these acres is heard any voice
But voice of cold water that runs here and there
Through rocks and lank heather growing without care.
No mice in heath run, no song-birds fly
For fear of the buzzard that floats in the sky.

Robert Graves

ANCIENT FOREST LAWS

The word "forest" is used throughout this book to mean a hunting reserve and not an area of woodland. One of the definitions of "forest" in the Oxford Dictionary is "a wild uncultivated waste" while Chambers defines it as "a royal preserve for hunting, governed by a special code called The Forest Law". In a court case in 1688, the following definition was given:

> Forests are waste grounds belonging to the King, replenished with all manners of beasts of chase or venery [practice of hunting] which are under the King's protection and for the sake of his royal recreation and delight; and to that end, and for preservation of the King's game, there are particular laws, privileges, courts and officers.[1]

Under Scots law, forest land was originally restricted to the King and applied to land reserved for keeping deer and for hunting purposes. However, during the Middle Ages this privilege was extended to noble families and thereafter royal and baronial forests became widespread. Atholl was a baronial forest and was managed according to special regulations based upon forest laws.

By Roman law, the chase was "free to all men"[2] and wild animals belonged to the person who first seized them, whether they were found on his own land or on that of a neighbour. No one was allowed to enter another person's land for the purpose of sport and pleasure and if he did so, he was liable to harsh penalties. After the Norman Conquest all hunting rights were held by the King and this was enforced with the utmost vigour in these ancient forests, where vast tracts of land were reserved solely for royal enjoyment and sometimes the death penalty was imposed on anyone caught hunting in them. These draconian measures were gradually eased over the ensuing centuries and eventually many forests were stripped of these oppressive laws. Under English forest law the penalties were extremely harsh with punishments such as castration, loss of eyes and the cutting off of hands and feet as some of the risks gambled with by poachers.[3]

Scottish Laws

The forest laws of Scotland in the Middle Ages were different from those in England and under the title "Hunting within the King's Forests", there were a number of provisions:

1. If anyone hunts within the King's forest without a licence, he should pay £10.

2. If any tenant lets his hounds follow deer into the King's forest, he may follow as far as he can throw his horn or his dog leash.

3. If it happens that the hounds kill a beast, the tenants shall take the animals "without challenge of anie man".

4. If in following his hounds he exceeds the limit, he shall remove his bow and arrows and bind them together with the bow string. If the hounds have killed the beasts, he shall "pass away quite and free".[4]

Two Atholl hounds bred specially to hunt deer.

These laws show that anyone who commenced hunting on his own land was perfectly entitled to follow the quarry across the boundary and enter the King's forest. Different laws were imposed in those forests belonging to barons such as Atholl and under the title "Trespass committed within Forests pertaining to Baronies", the following laws applied:

1. If any man commits a trespass in a forest belonging to a baron, he is fined £10, which is paid to the King.

2. The lord of the forest shall confiscate the hunter's horse and is empowered to strip him of all his possessions.

3. In the event of the lord not prosecuting an offender for trespass, the King is still entitled to a fine of £10 for "breaking of his command".[5]

Oldest Statute

One of the oldest statutes on this subject appeared in an Act by King James 1 in 1424:

> It is ordained that the Justice-clerke sall inquire of stalkers that flayis deare, that is to say, harte [stag], hynde, dae [doe] and rae [roe] and the halders and mainteiners of them, and alsoone as onie stalker may be convict of slaughter of deer, he sall paie to the King fourtie shillings: And the halders and mainteiners of them sall paie ten poundes.[6]

This statute prohibiting the killing of deer was absolute and applied universally to everyone in the country. It was a form of conservation as deer stocks were dwindling at that time. In the same year an Act was passed forbidding the hunting of wild-fowl (game-birds) between Lent and August "under the penalty of fourtie shillings" and again this was more in the nature of a conservation measure.[7] Partridges, plovers, black cock, grouse and other game birds were included in this prohibition. In 1457 no-one was permitted to kill wild-fowl at moulting time since "they could not fly" and this Act also offered protection to pheasants, cranes, herons and quails. Parliament gave further protection to wild ducks and partridges in 1474 by making the theft of their eggs a punishable offence and the heron was given total protection in 1793 as it was "reserved to the King".[8]

Another Act was passed in 1474 forbidding the hunting of deer "in time of storme or snaw, or slaie onie of their kidds, qhil they be ane zeir auld".[9] In addition, anyone found hunting for deer in a park was "punished as a thief". Again, this act was universal and applied to everyone except Keepers of Royal Forests, one of whom, by this time, was the Earl of Atholl, who was granted royal powers associated with hunting. An Act of 1551 forbade anyone "to shute at deere, rae, or other wild beasts, or wild fowls, with half hag, culvering [hand gun] or pistolet, in onie time to come, under the pain of death and confiscation of all their goods for their contempion".[10]

An Act passed in the reign of Mary Queen of Scots in 1555 decreed that:

> Na man take upon hand to ride or gang into their neighbours corns in Haulking or Hunting frae the Feast of Pasche [Easter] unto the time that the samen be shorn, And that na man ride nor gang upon wheat na time of the year, And that na Pettrick [partridge] be taken unto the Feast of Michaelmas [29 September], and that na person range other mens Woods, Parks, Hainings [enclosures] within Dykes without licence of the owner of the Ground Under the pain of refundment of the damage and Skaith [injury] to the party upon whose corns they gang, or ride or whose Woods, Parks, Hainings within Dykes they shall happen to range, And ten pounds for the first fault to our Sovereign Ladie, £20 the next and the third fault escheiting [removing] of their goods moveable.[11]

This Act related only to ground enclosed by dykes (walls) and anyone caught offending three times had all his goods and property taken away. It was decreed in 1621 that "no man hunt nor hawk at any time thereafter, who hath not a plough of land in heritage under the pains of ane hundred pounds".[12] A ploughland was a measurement of land equalling eight oxgangs, each one containing up to thirteen acres of cultivable ground. This was a very short statute,

Grouse in flight in an Atholl forest. (Roger Lee, Calvine)

which was in effect a disarming act designed to "keep the rusticae in as low a condition as possible and especially to prohibit them the use of arms".

Two partridges, which appear as "pettrick" in old manuscripts.
(Roger Lee)

Game Preservation

A Mutual Obligation was drawn up in 1630 between the Earl of Atholl and two of his neighbours, the Marquis of Huntly and the Earl of Mar, "for preserving the deer and game within their forests". They agreed that their forests had been "greatumlie waisted and abused be Foulares and Shuteares with gunnes" and in consequence, game was becoming scarce. Their remedy was to apprehend anyone found in their respective forests, confiscate their dogs, nets and guns and exact a fine of £20.[13]

A royal commission signed by King Charles II on 19 September 1675, granted "full power to John Earl of Atholl to pass, search, seek and take and apprehend the said persons contraveners of our said Act of Parliament wherever they can be found and apprehended".[14] This commission was specifically aimed at anyone caught killing deer without permission and in effect gave the Earl royal powers for the detection and punishment of offenders.

"Taking to their consideration the great decay of game in this his ancient Kingdom", King James VII and II passed a law in 1685 which decreed that gamekeepers should apprehend anyone they found in the forests with guns and dogs and take them to the nearest Sheriff Office for questioning. The reason for this was that it was considered that "setting dogs and other Engynes for killing of fowles is a great cause of the scarcety of game". No one was allowed in the forests without express permission from a landlord who had a minimum annual rental of £1,000. Anyone caught without this authority was liable to six weeks in prison and have their dogs and guns confiscated.[15]

King James VII succeeded to the throne in February 1685, at a time when the Scottish nation was being cruelly oppressed and persecuted. Alarmed by the prospect of riots, the government resorted to this new game law, hiding behind the pretence of the preservation of wild game, as it was declared at the time that "there is not only danger of an utter decay of so useful creatures but the manly exercise of hunting and hawking is like to be altogether neglected". Under this pretext, therefore, all the former game laws were revived but its real use and object was effectively to disarm the bulk of the country, leaving landowners with an annual rental income of £1,000 Scots (£83.6.8 Sterling) as the only people entitled to hunt.

[43 & 44 VICT.]   *Ground Game Act*, 1880.   [CH. 47.]

CHAPTER 47.

An Act for the better protection of Occupiers of Land against A.D. 1880. injury to their Crops from Ground Game.

[7th September 1880.]

More statutes followed, ostensibly in the interests of conservation and the thirteenth Act of Queen Anne's parliament in 1707 legislated that:

> No common fowler shall presume to hunt on any grounds without a subscribed warrant from the Proprietors of the said grounds under the Penalty of £20 toties besides forfeiting their dogs, guns and nets to the apprehenders or discoverers. And it is hereby further provided that no Fowler or any other person whatsoever shall come within any Heritors ground without leave asked and given by the Heritor with setting dogs and nets for killing fowles by nets. And if any common fowler shall be found in any place with guns or nets having no licence from any Nobleman or heritor they shall be sent abroad as recruits. As also that no person whatsoever shall shoot hares under the foresaid penalty of £20 toties ...[16]

This related solely to "common fowlers" who used nets to trap their quarry, resulting in the virtual cessation of this practice by the second half of the eighteenth century. Throughout the eighteenth and nineteenth centuries various acts were passed in an effort to counter illegal hunting and to preserve certain wild life which was in danger of becoming extinct. Item six under the 1880 Ground Game Act specifically related to hares and rabbits, decreeing that nobody had a right to kill this game between one hour after sunset and one hour before sunrise. The use of poison and traps, except in rabbit holes, was forbidden.[17]

SHIELINGS

The Atholl deer forests abound in shieling remains - there were over a hundred of them - and their green pasture provided excellent grazing for tenants' livestock throughout the summer months. Shielings are found where climate or topography cause a seasonal variation in the availability of pasture, so that man and his herds must move their base at least twice a year to win maximum use from the land. Only where the countryside is suitable for grazing, for at least part of the year and impracticable for conversion to cultivable land, would a shieling system exist. Such conditions were to be found in the Scottish Highlands, where the grazing grounds and bothies high up in the mountains were known as shielings.[18]

Transhumance

The practice of transhumance, the seasonal movement of livestock, began when tilling the soil started, as livestock had to be removed to a safe distance from crops under cultivation. This was an integral part of every community where crop growing was balanced with animal husbandry. The earliest shielings were located in the foothills but as pressure for space for people and their crops increased, these well-manured grazing areas became sites for permanent farms, so that the shieling sites were moved higher up the glens. The shieling bothies required annual repairs as they were rough, low-roofed erections of turf and stone, with no windows but only a door in the centre and a hole in the roof to serve as a chimney. They were occupied by old women, wives, sisters and children, with their simple furniture consisting of two or three seats made from turf and stone, a bed raised off the floor on a base of turf and simple utensils of wood and earthenware. A milk-house and small hut or shelter for young calves was often attached to the bothy, while occasionally a stone enclosure was built, within which efforts to grow a few potatoes and a little oats were made.[19]

Grazing Laws

The grazing of livestock on mountain pastures was in conflict with deer forest activities, so that early forest laws imposed strict regulations to ensure that the full enjoyment of the chase was not impaired:

Sheep: Concerning sheep found in the forest, the forester can take one sheep from the flock for his own use when trusty witnesses have been brought as to whether or not a herdsman was present.

Goats: Concerning goats found in the forest it is lawful for the forester on each of three occasions to hang one of them by the horns and on the fourth occasion he ought to kill one of them and leave its entrails there as a sign they were found there.

Pigs: Concerning pigs the custom is that in parish churches they should be publicly prohibited from entering the forest and should they be found after this prohibition, it is lawful for the forester on each of three occasions to take one

An early twentieth century photograph of a cow being milked in front of a shieling bothy, a low-roofed erection of turf and stone. A creel for carrying peat lies on the roof.

of them for his own use and if they enter the forest a fourth time, let them all be taken for the King's use.

Horses: Concerning horses it is lawful for the forester to take a one-year-old foal the first time, a two-year-old the second time and a three-year-old the third time and if they are found a fourth time, the whole stud will be taken for the King's use.[20]

As early as the fifteenth century, records show that attempts were made to pasture cattle clandestinely in the forest but this was not without its problems either. Anyone found trespassing was not only seized, and their livestock impounded but they ran the risk of being "carried off by the Freebooters (called Katharin), hordes of whom infested the surrounding mountains and frequently came down and swept the country of everything of any value".[21] To put a stop to this, the Earl of Atholl sometimes paid for his tenants to pasture their livestock near his forests, provided they prevented these predatory incursions. A further measure was instituted in 1594 when Alastair McIntosh was granted a shieling and full powers to prevent incursions:

> ... giffis libertie to our Lovit Servitur Allester McIntoische in Terein [Tirinie] to scheill and pastur his awin guidis allenarlie this present summer and forder induring our Will in quatsumever pairts of the bounds of or glane that our burnen or oney ane of thane pastouris zair guidis in prowyding that neither he nor they pastor zair guidis nor scheill aboun Poltary as also that the said Allester as he is already bound to us keep our Dier from skerring slaying or any other inconvenientes...[22]

The Seventeenth Century

By the middle of the seventeenth century cattle rearing was becoming more productive and many parts of the deer forests provided ideal pasture land in the summer months. Shielings therefore developed along the outskirts of forest land as a method of preventing the illegal use of forest pasture and preserving the boundaries from the encroachment of neighbouring people from Mar and Badenoch. In the absence of boundary dykes, shieling tenants provided a useful means of guarding and patrolling the frontiers of the deer forests. To safeguard not only the forests but also to ensure that deer suffered minimum disturbance, tenants were given a "bare servitude of pasturage" of their shielings and were sometimes required to move to an alternative grazing area if their particular shieling was deemed "prejudicial to the forest".

According to the Earl of Atholl, a number of tenants were abusing the system, so in 1668 he issued various orders concerning the preservation of his deer forests and compelled the following tenants to sign in compliance: John Robertson, Fornoch; John Stewart, Croft Crombie; Alexander Stewart, Orchilbeg; William Mackintosh, Tirinie; Allan Stewart, Strathgarry.

Two drovers with Highland cattle in the nineteenth century.

These tenants agreed that:

> ... for taking notice of such persones as resorts in pasturing with thair goods and bestialles in his Lordship's forests in Atholl, and in obedience thereto I the said John Robertsone binds and obleisses me, my aires, executoures and assignais, and inacting my selff under the penultie of the somme of ane hunderyth merkes, toties, to keip, detein absent and nor to trouble nor molest with my saides goodes and bestialles furth from the day and date of thir presentes his Lordship's forrest ...[23]

A constant feature of deer forests throughout the centuries was the conflict between hunting reserves and agricultural interests. It was generally true that an area could not be maintained solely as a hunting reserve when it was subjected to continuous pressure from such shieling activities as the grazing of large numbers of livestock.

TINCHELS

No conventional methods of hunting, as practised in more gentle terrain, were possible in much of the wilderness of the rock and bog of the Atholl deer forest, because no horseman could travel fast enough across the rough landscape. The answer to this was the tinchel which was a system of driving herds of deer to an appointed place where there was some form of enclosure, known as an Elrig and an indication of their whereabouts in Atholl, lingers in some of the place names as follows:

Elrig Bheithe (enclosure of birch trees) 804 669 and **Elrig na Curigin** 762 662, are both in the Clunes forest. **Elrig an Righ** (enclosure of the king) 832 691; **Elrig** (deer enclosure) 871 725 and **Elrig'ic an Toisich** (McIntosh's enclosure) 867 789, all lie in the West Hand forest. **Ruidh na h-Elrig** (shieling of the enclosure) 970 707 lies in the Seven Shielings forest and **Elrig** (deer enclosure) 918 697 is in Lude forest.

To form a tinchel, large numbers of men, sometimes several hundred, were called out to make a ring of several miles in diameter, and having completed the cordon, the beaters gradually drove the deer inwards, forcing them together and pushing them towards the ambush. Here the Earl of Atholl and his hunting friends, all armed, were waiting at the enclosure which was formed by barricades on three sides and often located at the junction of two rivers. At the last moment there was a brief and bloodthirsty massacre when the hounds were unleashed and the hunters flung themselves on the trapped deer with any weapon they could muster: bow and arrow, sword, dirk, spear, axe or stone. The climax of a tinchel must have exhibited, to our eyes, a very barbaric, frenzied slaughter. There is an old account of how both John Robertson of Eastertyre and John Stewart of Blair Atholl each cut a stag clean in half with a single blow of their broadswords.

James Robertson, who was a minister in

Ruidh na h-Elrig, shieling of the deer enclosure, probably on the site of a tinchel, with Carn nan Gabhar, the highest mountain in Atholl, as a backdrop.

A hunting party returning to Blair Castle in 1862. After the 1745 rising the castle was demilitarised with two upper floors removed so that it resembled a large Georgian house. (William Evans, Eton)

Two Highland ponies, "Kitty" and "Steelie", returning to Blair Castle with their ponyman and deer hounds, after a hunt in 1850. (William Evans)

H.R.H. Prince Waldemar of Prussia spent a few days at Blair in 1847. On 19 August he shot his first stag and this painting shows the shooting party fording the Tilt. (William Evans)

Two of the Duke of Atholl's deer-hounds.

George Fraser, son of Peter Fraser the head keeper, with two deer-hounds in 1856. (William Evans)

Callander, gives a vivid description of a tinchel at the end of the eighteenth century in his *General View of the Agriculture in the County of Perth*:

> While the deer were permitted to inhabit the vallies, and the country was under wood, the natives hunted them, by surrounding them with men, or by making large inclosures of such a height as the deer could not overleap, fenced with stakes and entwined with brush wood. Vast multitudes of men were collected on hunting days, who forming a ring round the deer, drove them into these inclosures, which were open on one side. From some eminence, which overlooked the inclosure, the principal personages and others, who did not choose to engage in the chace, were spectators of the whole diversion. These inclosures were called in the language of the country elerig which is derived from another word that signifies contest or strife ...

Sometimes a tinchel was not as innocent as it appeared to be, as under the pretext of forming a hunting party, chiefs would call their men together to raid a neighbouring clan. The formation of the genuine hunting tinchel required very careful planning and every autumn the Duke summoned his Fencible men, that is those aged between sixteen and fifty who were fit for military service. He also invited friends, and perhaps those whom he wished to impress, to attend, of whom many did, but some, like the Earl of Strathmore, declined, as his letter of 14 September 1704, written from Castle Lyon (now Castle Huntly), shows:

> May it please Your Grace
> I came to this place with a full designe to have watched you att your hunting but yesterday I was taken ill with a kind of Aguish distemper which obliges me to take some rest and keep home. This I much more regret since I cannot promise to be with you. If any of your people could possibly save a young hart or two alive soe as I could get them brought here I shall take it as a favour and send for them for that kind is wearing out here and I am loath they should.[24]

A second refusal for the same tinchel came from the Earl Marischal at Fetteresso:

> ... I have a relevant excuse when I do not perform what I promise to Your Grace when I proposed the honour of waiting on you and the best sport I can imagine. But have been so ill with pains in my stomach that I am yet scarce able to stir abroad and I am afraid the hunting will be over before I am in a condition to travell. I need not wish you good sport for I believe Your Grace is prob[abl]y sure of it with your good weather...[25]

Instructions

In August 1710 the Duke of Atholl issued orders to his vassals and tenants to be "at their place on Tuesday 22nd of this instant in the evening with their best arms and apparell as is usual and six days provisions to attend us at a deerhunt..."[26]

The result of one of Walter Winans' deer drives in Glen Tilt in 1871 · 17 stags brought down with the support of many keepers and ponies. This was reminiscent of the great tinchels of the previous century.

Notices to this effect were posted on church doors and a large body of men assembled on the Green, east of the Mains of Blair beside Blair Castle, where a number of instructions were read out to the gathering:

> 1. That no one shall offer to fire a gun or pistol in time of the deer hunting.
>
> 2. That none shall offer to break up a deer or take out a gralloch except in His Grace's presence where they are to be disposed of.
>
> 3. That none to be drunk or swear an oath.
>
> Whosoever shall transgress any of the said rules shall be fyned and taken in custody.[27]

Despite these warnings and restrictions, tinchels were accompanied by much good humour and drinking. There was even a report which alleged that after a hunt in 1704, the Duke drank out of Bonnie Dundee's skull, which caused something of a scandal. Invitations to attend a hunt in 1711 were again issued to friends and neighbours, one of whom, David Spalding of Ashintully, replied on 21 August:

> In obedience to Your Grace desyre I have sent about an hundereth men to Your Grace hunting, which is all possible for me to get appoynted in cloathes and armes, considdering the short advertisement, for I only receaved Your Grace Letter on Sabbath, which if I had got sooner I would have endeavoured to have sent als many againe and would have waited on Your Grace myself, according to my deutie, wer it not that I have been tender of a long tym, soe that I cannot traivell without my hurt and prejudice.[28]

This hunt started on 22 August in the Beinn a' Ghlo mountains where no deer were killed. Next day in the Fealar forest, twenty five were killed and on Ben Vuirich the following day a total of thirty two were slaughtered. The Atholl invitation to a tinchel always included instructions to bring as many "goode dogis" as possible, as the sport could not take place without them. By the beginning of the eighteenth century these great deer hunts were taking place less frequently, not only because of general advances being made in agriculture, but also because it was proving more difficult to muster hundreds of men to man the ring. Atholl, however, still maintained the tradition of and supremacy in the sport, until at least 1800, when records show that a line of about four miles was manned by two hundred men. On that occasion about 1,200 deer were surrounded but the vast majority escaped, with only a kill of six being recorded.

A stag scene in Glenshee. (Roger Lee)

ATHOLL DEER FORESTS

A legal document from the 1850s contains a vivid description of the Atholl deer forests in the seventeenth century:

> The Forests of Athole are of great extent comprehending many miles of the wild romantic and mountainous district of the Highlands of Perthshire. They extend from Aberdeenshire and the hills of Glenshee on the east to the hills beyond the Water of Garry on the west and from Blair Athole on the south to the boundaries of the Counties of Aberdeen and Inverness on the north and contain a space of about 24 miles by 10 or nearly one hundred and fifty thousand acres and composes the three great forests of Athole called the East the Middle and the West forests.

> These forests from their wild and inaccessible character in former times, when the rearing of sheep and cattle was almost impractible and the higher districts were chiefly valuable as a haunt for deer and other beasts and fowls of the forest for the protection of which the rights of free forestry were granted to the ancestors of the Memorialist [Atholl]. Besides the rights of free forestry however the Memorialist's ancestors were in use to receive special Royal Commissions arming them with all the powers of Royalty for the more summary and effectual detection and punishment of offenders against the Acts of Parliament anent the killing and slaying of deer.[1]

Early Forests

In the early days, the Atholl deer forest was placed under the charge of vassals and tenants having land adjacent to them but by the seventeenth century it had been effectively divided into three separate forests. On 30 May 1637 Angus McIntosh of Tirinie was given charge of the East forest of Benechrombie (Fealar), with powers to impound "all lowland oxen, stirks [one-to-two-year-old cattle], staigis [stallions] ye can apprehend within our saide forrestis and put the samen in puind fauldis [poind folds] or bring the samen to our Castle of Blair".[2]

Another commission was granted to Patrick Robertson to be gamekeeper of the Middle and West forests, "with full power to seize and apprehend the dogs, guns or nets of any person who shall attempt to hunt or shoot within the saide forrestis".[3]

By the early eighteenth century there were four separate forests in Atholl, as follows:

1. The forest of Freechrombie, now known as the Seven Shielings, which measured about six miles by eight miles and was centred on Loch Loch. In 1707, Thomas Mackenzie from Rienakyllich was appointed gamekeeper of this hunting reserve

An aerial view of Fealar Lodge.

Grouse in flight at the south end of Loch Loch. (Roger Lee)

and in additon to his wage, "for his encouragement" was permitted to kill a deer a year for his own use, along with any lame ones he found. His instructions were:

> ... to kill fifteen Deer yearly for our [the Duke's] use. You are to take particular care to preserve the Deer in our said forest and for that end you are carefully and exactly to observe keep and perform all and every of the proceeding instructions relative hereto. And to assist the rest of our forresters when there is occasion ...[4]

Thomas was allowed to pasture his cattle in **Ruidh Mor Fealar** 997 793, a shieling in the Fealar forest. A year later he was joined by Donald Flemming from Glenshee.

2. The Tarf forest, ten miles in length, lies between the Tilt and the Bruar with the county

Rienakyllich, the home of Thomas Mackenzie, who was in charge of the Seven Shielings in the early 1700s.

march as its northern boundary. Alexander Stewart from Innerslanie in Glen Tilt was appointed gamekeeper there, with the additional responsibility of the Beinn a' Ghlo reserve, which was about twenty miles round. His instructions were to kill twenty deer a year for castle consumption, while he was permitted to take two deer a year for himself, along with any lame ones he found.[5] He was allocated a shieling near the head of Glen Tilt called **Ruidh Leth-Chois** 985 799, where the remains of several shieling bothies are still clearly visible. Alexander Stewart was cited in a forest abuse case in 1704 as this shieling was regarded as one of the most damaging to deer, being the place where hinds were accustomed to calve. An eye-witness declared that before the shieling was built, he had seen more than 1,000 hinds there, but thereafter there were not even fifty.

3. Part of Glen Garry between Bruar Water and the Edendon Water, eighteen miles across and eight miles in depth, up to the county march with Inverness-shire formed the third forest. James Robertson of Calvine was appointed in charge and "for his encouragement and pains" was given the shieling at Sronphadruig. Donald Kerr, his servant, became his assistant with orders from the Duke to kill deer for the castle, as needed. His instructions were "to take the arms from such persons as travail through the said forest either killing Deer, Roe or wild fowl, and to apprehend the persons themselves and bring them prisoner to us. And to give up the names of

all those you shall hear tell of to kill Deer, Roe or wild fowl ..."[6]

4. The West forest of Glen Garry, covered about eight miles from the Edendon Water to the County March with Inverness at Drumochter. Patrick Robertson of Blairfettie was given the responsibility for this part. He, along with his son, James, Donald Robertson of Auchleeks and his son, Patrick, Alexander Robertson of Drumachine and James Robertson of Calvine were given added powers to control drovers using the military road through the glen. They were to exact a fine of 12d Scots (1 penny Sterling) for each cow and ox travelling from the north to the trysts at Comrie and Falkirk, resting for the night on Atholl property.

James Ban Robertson, a servant of the Duke, was appointed gamekeeper in the Atholl deer forest with a roving commission to come and go where he pleased and was empowered to apprehend any lowland oxen or swine he found grazing in the forest and to impound them. He was also asked to report any instances of muir burning that took place and inform "our Baillies of the raisers of the same that they may be fyned by them according to Law". Around this time, Lord James Murray of Garth, third son of the first Marquis, was appointed head gamekeeper in overall charge of all the forests of Atholl. He was given powers to "call on our Forresters to account how they observe, keep and perform all and every of the instructions given them with

their commissions, what care they take to preserve the deer in their respective forests and how they perform their duties in keeping the marches of the forrests, killing their respective numbers of deer for our use ..."[7]

Keepers' Instructions

As the organisation of the forests gathered pace at the start of the eighteenth century, the foresters (gamekeepers) themselves were given very strict instructions, covering every conceivable situation, under a command headed:

Instructions given by ane High and Mighty John Duke of Atholl to his Grace's fforesters of the fforestrie of Atholl. July 6th 1706.

1. They shall neither kill deer nor roe to themselves, nor to any other person whatsoever without a special warrand.

2. They shall neither see nor hear tell of any person, or persons to kill deer or roe or wild fowl within any part of the fforests without revealing the name to the said Duke.

3. They shall not suffer any stranger or countryman to shoot guns or hang butts [hagbuts] within any part of the fforests without apprehending them and taking their guns from them.

4. They take particular care that no swine be pastured in the fforest.

5. They strictly keep the marches and meiths [boundary stones] against all persons and suffer

Ruidh Leth-Chois, the shieling at the head of Glen Tilt where hinds were accustomed to calve, was given to Alexander Stewart, the Tarf keeper in 1707.

Neil McBeath. Donald Rose. Robert Stewart. Robt. McNaughton. Wm McAra. Peter McDuff.
Wm Campbell. John Robertson. Alex. Gow. John Cameron. (Piper)
(Head Keeper) (2nd Piper) John Stewart. Alex McAra.
Dond McBeath. John McAra. Wm Ferguson. James McDonald. John McPherson. (Ex Head Forester)
(Head Forester) (Head Piper.)

Hillmen and keepers posing for the camera in Blair Castle grounds in 1868. Everyone is identified by the neat, hand-written caption.

none to pasture nor incroach upon the same.

6. They suffer no lowland oxen to pasture or feed within any part of the said fforest.

7. They take particular care and notice of any horses and mares within the fforest and suffer not any strayed horses or mares to pasture therein.

8. They frequently frequent and travell through the bounds of the fforests at all times of the year and shall not absent themselves from the said office except upon lawful occasions.

9. They shall not permitt any person whatsomever to possess any shealling in the fforest without his Grace's warrand in writing, except the tennents of the property.

10. They shall shoot any dogs they shall find within the ffforest in regard they scare the Deer and exact 20 shillings Scots from the master of every dog found there.

11. They kill or bring in alive any eagles old or young they can shoot or take in the fforest, and for their encouragement they shall have a warrand for killing a deer for their own use for each eagle old or young brought in by them.[8]

Gamekeepers were urged "carefully and exactly to observe, keep and perform all and every of the preceeding instructions" and to assist other keepers when called upon. As an incentive they were permitted to graze forty head of cattle on pasture agreed by the Duke, which would not be prejudicial to deer.

They were also told how many deer they should shoot each year, normally twenty, and were instructed to deliver them to Blair Castle, thus ensuring that none were retained for themselves. Deer had to be "sufficiently well grown for the Season" and for this they were paid twenty pounds Scots (£1.13.4 Sterling), with the added strong warning that for each additional deer they shot, there would be a fine of two pounds. This quota system changed in 1719 when instructions were given for as many deer as possible to be shot, at least two a week, and to assist them in bringing the deer to Blair, keepers were permitted "to take along with them a horse which they can feed on the best spot of grass they can find".[9]

Great care was needed to ensure that deer carcases were not damaged on their journey down the glen. The gamekeepers recorded all killings and had "to write down on a piece of paper the day and hour when any deer comes to Blair and in like manner the particular day and hour when the same are despatched". To ensure they arrived in the freshest possible condition, keepers were ordered not to "travel betwixt ten in the morning and four in the afternoon but wait till the heat of the day be over ..."[10]

The question of defining the marches of the forest of Atholl arose in 1717 when James Stewart, Chamberlain to the 1st Duke, assisted by Aeneas Macpherson of Killiehuntly in Badenoch, "called some of the most knowing men to the said march with other men, that they might know the said marches in time coming". A number of gamekeepers who attended this meeting on 16 August included: William MacIntosh and his son John from Cultmore; William's brother John in Dail Fheannach; John Stewart in Dail Mhorsaid; John Stewart, Pittinacy; John Stewart of Campsie; John Stewart from Blair; Robert Stewart in Blairuachter; John Gow in West Mains; Donald Stewart in Invervack; Thomas Stewart in Dalflachy; John Moon in Urrard More; Finlay Stewart there and Thomas Macpherson, servant of Aeneas Macpherson.[11]

Rights of Pasture

Tenants and vassals were accorded special rights of pasture and in 1708 were allowed to graze mares with up to three foals, the oldest not exceeding a year, mares being branded with the Atholl mark. They were also permitted to pasture their "riding" horses free and to kill game birds in any part of the forest. Those using guns and dogs had to provide twelve birds to the Duke, while six were required from those using a gun only.[12]

Such was the liberty given to gamekeepers and tenants to pasture their cattle that the estate became anxious about the damage being caused to the deer forests and alarmed as there was no profit from this practice for them. The estate maintained that: "the forest has been for sometime past, stockt with cattle without any profits to the Duke" and resolved to "preserve such parts of the forest as were the most proper and fitt nurserys for the deer".[13]

Alexander Stewart of Innerslanie and Patrick Robertson of Blairfettie, the two principal gamekeepers, were asked in 1726 to report on the state of the deer forests. Their recommendation was that no horses, nolts (black cattle), sheep and goats should graze in the deer nurseries and the use of shielings restricted to tenants only, their boundaries being strictly controlled. They also recommended that particular use of all the forests should be established:

EAST FOREST
Beinn a' Ghlo is to remain unchanged as it is unsuitable for shielings or the pasturing of cattle.
Beinn Vuirich (Seven Shielings) has no deer and could pasture one hundred cows.
Benechrombie with Fealar is very suitable for grazing four hundred cows.

NORTH FOREST
The Tarf is to be kept for deer only.

MID FOREST
Kirrachans (Clunes) are to continue as shielings as they are possessed by the lairds of Shierglas and Strathgarry.

"A Deer Herd crossing the Tilt".

Peter Fraser as a young keeper.

Glaschoire (Dalnamein) are shielings for the lairds of Fincastle and Bonskeid.

WEST FOREST

Sronphadruig is to be kept for deer. The lands from Edendon Water west to Drumochter are suitable for fattening three hundred cows. Dalnaspidal is to be kept strictly for deer.

The outcome of the above proposals was that the keepers were invited to make a money offer for their grazings in the Atholl forests. Stewart immediately proposed £400 Scots (£33.6.8 Sterling) for the East forest, which was capable of pasturing 500 cattle, on condition that the existing tenant was removed. This man, a shepherd called Bennet, said that a quarter of the area would be sufficient for his needs and offered £200 Scots (£16.13.4 Sterling), thereby implying that the whole area should be worth £800 Scots and that Stewart's offer was derisory. Patrick Robertson of Blairfettie indicated that it was too late in the season for him to make changes and asked to continue with his shielings in Dalnaspidal. The Mid forest, capable of holding 200 cows, was already leased to Patrick McGlashan, the Blair Atholl miller and this arrangement could not in the meantime be altered. The estate considered all these points and decided they could not pass judgment until they had visited the forests "with skilful and honest men". They also felt that the season was too far advanced to make any alterations that year and therefore decided to leave Bennet alone but restrict him to a quarter of the Fealar forest.[14]

Diminishing Power

Over the years the powers of these gamekeepers gradually diminished from being empowered in 1706 to arrest people, confiscate their guns and shoot dogs on sight, to 1750, by which time they were restricted to only seizing the guns of anyone caught hunting and could not confiscate grazing animals. By 1767 the Duke's minions had instructions to be even more cautious in their manner when encountering strangers in the forest, as orders given to them in that year enjoined them:

> ... carefully to watch His Grace's grounds in their severall districts and when they observe any person or persons coming to hunt there with dogs, guns or nets, they are to order matters so that a clear proof may be brought by the testimony of two concerning witnesses ... who can swear to the identity of the person, that they saw him shoot and saw his dog sett in the field, no matter whether he miss or kill. And for the greater certainty the gamekeeper or servants who watch the ground after hearing or seeing one shott, are in a discreet way to talk to the person or persons that was shooting or hunting and let him or them know whose ground they were hunting on, that they are by their master ordered to watch and ask their names in a civill way that they may report to their master for their own exoneration least they lose their bread.[15]

One reason for this more circumspect approach was the erosion of the powers of the old Baron Courts after 1748, when landowners and barons like the Dukes of Atholl lost judicial power over their people and they became far less sure of their legal ground. Indeed, despite many

Assembling for a day's covert shooting on 31 October 1867 outside the old front door of the castle.

historical precedents, no one was absolutely sure to whom the deer belonged. In view of all this uncertainty, it is hardly surprising that poachers co-operated even less when challenged by gamekeepers.

Pheasants

Captive rearing of pheasants commenced in the 1750s and by 1761 forty one were hatched, of which sixteen were released in the beginning of September. Of these, two cocks and four hens were taken to "the little house over against the cascades in Toldamdh", where John Muckle gave them food and water for two days, after which time they were set free. Throughout the winter the hut doors were left open so that the birds could come and go as they pleased, with food being provided for them. Another ten were released in Dunkeld. The remainder were kept in the pheasant house all winter and then let go, save for another two cocks and four hens which were kept back for further breeding purposes. The same numbers were reserved for Lord Breadalbane's estate at Taymouth.[16]

John Lightfoot from Bullstrode wrote to the Duke in November 1772, giving precise instructions as to the rearing of gold and silver pheasants as practised by the Duchess of Portland:

> In April the hens begin to lay. They make no nest but drop them upon the ground, one every morning or every other morning, to the number of ten or a dozen by each hen. The cock bird will suck the eggs as soon as they are laid if they are not carefully watched and instantly taken away. The hen is never allowed to sit on her own eggs but when she has laid her numbers, they must be placed under a common domestic hen.

> The eggs of the gold pheasant will be hatched in three weeks, of the silver in three weeks and three days. As soon as hatched the hen and young must be put in a kind of hatch. Their food from the time they are hatched, for two months to come, is either ant eggs which is their favourite food, or a stiff paste made of wheat flour and warm water which is broken into little bits and thrown before them. The red ants eggs are most proper at first but the great horse ants eggs will do when they grow more hardy.[17]

Reindeer

There was great excitement and anticipation in 1790, pending the arrival at Leith docks of seven reindeer, three males and four females from Archangel. George Farquhar, the Duke's Edinburgh agent, takes up the story on 30 August:

> I hired three men, careful and sober to guide the reindeer and lest any of them should sicken or die by the way, I sent a cart enlarged by sparrs to attend them. My orders were to walk them very slowly and rest frequently, especially in the heat of the day. I put on the Cart 40 sixpenny loaves, a bag of rusks and a quantity of fresh hay. I accompanied them myself four miles and left them

well and hearty. I ordered them to stop at the ferry all night and not to exceed a few miles next day.

> Judge my feelings when late last night I received an express telling me that one buck and a doe were dead at a place called Croftgates [Crossgates], four miles beyond the ferry. I have ordered them to stop there and as soon as the present hurricane of wind abates a little so that I can get across the ferry, I shall set out and accompany them the rest of the way. The disappointment of part of my hopes, to put Your Grace in possession of what the King has often tried in vain to procure, cuts me to the bone. Had they been my own children I would not have taken more pains about them.[18]

George Farquhar, who lived in Edinburgh, caught up with the unfortunate party but in spite of his best efforts another doe died before they reached Dungarthill, to the east of Dunkeld. Soon after the survivors arrived at Blair Castle the old buck died and the remaining three were released to the Atholl hills "where they grow fat and seem to enjoy themselves and seem likely to thrive and do well". The Duke made several more attempts to import reindeer but, as with this one, they all ended in failure, and within two years all of them had died.

Capercaillie

In January 1824 the Duke received the gift of a capercaillie hen from Austria, which was the subject of much interest in the area, as these birds had been extinct in Scotland for forty five years. John Crerar, then head gamekeeper recorded the bird's progress through the regular reports he sent to the Duke:

> 8 January 1824
> Last Wednesday night Thomas Stewart came up here with a capercailie. It is a fine looking bird. It takes its meat very freely, picks the Juniper berries off the bushes neatly, and eats corn, barley, likewise it seems in excellent health. John Rusle is making a larger cage than the one it came in.[19]

A capercaillie in full display. (Roger Lee) Attempts to breed them in Atholl in the 1820s were unsuccessful.

16 January 1824
The capercailie is quite hearty and takes its food very well. John Rusle has made a larger cage in which I shall put her tomorrow morning.[20]

13 February 1824
The capercailie is in excellent health, its plumage is getting in order since it came and its beginning to look beautiful. Eats a vast amount of Juniper berries, those that are ripe and none of the green ones.[21]

6 June 1824
The capercailie has laid an egg yesterday (She was making a nest in the cage sum days before) of a redish colour with small brown spots.[22]

6 July 1824 - Duke's Journal
As a matter of great curiosity I must mention what at first will appear a very curious fact viz. that I eat two eggs of a capercailzie, laid by a hen which was sent me early in Spring. Unfortunately there was no cock sent. She has, however, at times laid several eggs - larger than a pheasant, and speckled brown and white, some a light chestnut brown. These eggs being of no use, I tasted them, and found them the finest eggs I have eat. I mean to eat two more, and blow two, which will account for all she has hitherto laid, and do my endeavor to procure a cock bird for next season.[23]

On 20 October 1825, Charles Mackintosh from the Crossmarket in Glasgow, sent the Duke a present of a capercaillie in the care of his servant, as a mate for the hen he already possessed.

23 May 1826 John Crerar
The capercailie is beginning to squat. I suppose she is having eggs as she used to do this before she has them.[24]

4 June 1826
The capercailie has begun laying. She has laid two but seems not so well as she used to be at this time.[25]

17 June 1826
The capercailie has laid five eggs. She was very restless all the time and I thought she could have gone ...[26]

28 July 1826 (to James Stewart, House Steward)
As I am not able to move upon my legs to go so far as the house, I send the capercailie's six eggs. Let His Grace know that the first egg was hatched [laid] about the 1st of June, and there has been about ten days and a fortnight betwixt each egg. The hen was taken badly yesterday morning hatching [laying] another egg, but cannot get it away, and I rather think it will be her if not soon hatched [laid]. She has been worse this year than former times hatching [laying].[27]

The capercaillie died soon after and it was not until 1837 that these birds were successfully re-introduced to Scotland by Lord Breadalbane at Taymouth.

Deer-hounds

All hunts, large or small, depended on hounds which were of two types: those which hunted by sight and those which approached their quarry by scent. Sighting hounds were essential for tinchels, whereas stalking required the use of hounds that hunted by scent. Many hounds were bred on the estate but sometimes they were the gift of friends as we can see from this letter from Joseph Stewart of Foss to the Atholl factor in 1804:

> When I had the pleasure of seeing you last harvest you seemed to think that the old dog Nelson would be of use to his Grace as a breeder. I have recovered him lately from North Uist and have taken the liberty to send him by the bearer to McIntyre's care [Forest Lodge]. He is quite fresh, and I think will be able to run down many harts when the season commences.[28]

Such a gift was not always welcome, however, as one of John Crerar's reports in 1826 shows:

> The other day Mr Butter of Faskally send a very fine looking black greyhound down here for Your Grace since Mr Butter called here and told me he was a present from Mr John Menzies to Your Grace. I told him as the dog being strange and in but one place, the other dogs would likely kill him.[29]

One of John Crerar's duties was the feeding of the hounds and an 1827 report records how this was done:

> We have been getting as many useless horses for the dogs as we could. I sent Fraser to Stanley last week for a horse. He boils them with potatoes and a little meal and makes good food and since we have been getting the horse flesh it saves just one half meal when horse flesh can be got.[30]

The value of meal fed to dogs in 1826 was as follows:[31]

	Bolls	Firlots	Pecks
Deer Hounds at Blair	12	3	2
Dunkeld	22	1	3
Pointers at Blair	8	2	2
Dunkeld	20	0	3
Fox Hounds	19	3	3
	84	0	1

These weights conformed to the Linlithgow System, a medieval form of volumetric measurement devised for millers. A boll was equivalent to about ten stone (140 lb) by volume; four firlots equalled one boll and four pecks were the equivalent of one firlot. At £1 per boll, the cost of feeding the Atholl hounds in a year was £84.1.3.

Deer Antlers

In John Crerar's report of 5 April 1822, he noted that "the harts are dropping there horns very fast. The weather is favourable for them when they are dropping them, being fine dry clear weather".[32] The estate, however, particularly the keepers, frowned upon the practice of horn collecting, as they often had a ready market for them. John Walker, the ground officer, noted down the names of those seen gathering up antlers in Glen Tilt and reported them to the factor. The offenders were:

1st May: Isobel Cameron, Haugh of Blair
Janet Stewart, Haugh of Blair

3rd May: Janet Stewart, Lambton
Finlay Cameron, Lambton, with a dog
John Hay, son to the Minister's tenant[33]

The Duke naturally wanted the best horn for his own use, as is shown in a letter his house steward wrote to John Crerar on 19 February 1818:

> His Grace wishes some of the best deer hornes to be sent to London for knife handles. I beg leave to request you will please to order some of the best to be picked out, say 12 heads, that His Grace can select the handsomest for the above purpose.[34]

A Day with the Duke

In *The Driffield Angler*, written by Alexander Mackintosh, there is a description of a day spent by the author in the Atholl deer forests in the early part of the nineteenth century:

> I had the honour to attend the Duke of Athol on an excursion into his extensive forest in August, 1805, and shall here attempt to describe the manner of his grace's sport: when he first alights from his horse the servants present him with telescopes, by the use of which, looking on the mountains' sides, or in the valleys, it is easy to distinguish every hart, hind or calf; and I may venture to say that in eight hours not fewer have been perceived than from three to four thousand head, young and old, in a corner of the forest; and were it possible to go over it in one day, I am confident a man might see, at least, ten thousand deer.
>
> When his grace espies the harts lying down, or grazing, he uses all methods to gain the wind of them, approaching with the utmost caution till within a hundred or six score yards, he fires from a rifle gun, and being a capital marksman seldom misses his aim; as the herd passes by his servants supply him with a second and third piece, and he frequently kills a hart at each shot. When they are not to be come in at the wide and open valleys, his men are sent round in all directions where the deer can catch the wind of them, and on sight, or winding of them, the deer turn down wind, where his grace, taking advantage of the track with the wind in his favour in the time they drive by him, can fire the three rifle guns in one minute, and will hit them on full speed from one hundred to one hundred and fifty yards distance. When the deer is wounded, in a general way, he leaves the herd, or rather the other harts force him out as soon as he begins to bleed freely. The man who leads the greyhounds, by a signal from his grace's hand, uncouples one or both of them, when they come to his grace, or the forester, the dog or dogs are laid to the slot, or track; if the deer has not broke from the herd, the greyhounds will single him out from the others if there be a thousand of them together, and will not look at any other but that deer which is wounded: sometimes he will run a mile or two before the dogs bring him to bay, there they will keep him till the forester comes up and cuts the deer's throat, and the dogs reward is the hot blood, which makes them eager and keen.

The English Invasion

By the start of the nineteenth century a number of shooting lodges had been built in various parts of the Atholl deer forests and within twenty years there was an ever-increasing demand for shooting lets, particularly from England. So popular had the Scottish moors and forests become by 1840, that newspapers carried reports of many hopeful sportsmen who had "to return south after travelling over the whole of the north in search of shooting quarters without being able to obtain a nook or cranny". This became known as "The English Invasion".[35]

In those early days of shooting lets, sportsmen did not seek either large game bags or luxurious quarters. Some were content with a heather or turf-roofed hut, whilst others slept in shepherd's bothies or even in deserted shielings. Such conditions prevailed until the second half of the century, when lodges were extended and made more comfortable. Around this time there was a serious decline in the value of wool, so that many of the hill sheep farms were lying derelict. With the steadily increasing demand for access to the deer forests, the rise of the sporting tenant gradually replaced the hill shepherd and his flocks.

That the Atholl forest shooting grounds were well established by 1825, is shown in the following table:

List of Shooting Grounds reported to the Duke 25 February 1825[36].

GROUND	TENANT	RENT
Dalnaspidal	Col Paterson	£100
Dalnacardoch	Mr Haig of Lochrin	£100
Struan Hill and Fishing	To let	£20
Clunes	To let	£40
Aldvouline	To let	£63
Bruar	William Scrope	£105
Fealar	Sir David Moncreiffe	£200
North Tarf	" " "	£100
Ben Vuirich	H. Hyett	£100
Bohespic and Strathtummel	To let	£25

By the end of the nineteenth century the shooting areas of Atholl were very similar to

A turf-roofed bothy, typical of a sportsman's accommodation in the early nineteenth century before shooting lodges were improved.

"The Start", first of four posed Victorian stalking scenes. A party of Scots Greys prepares for a day in the hills with their stalker and hound "Tulach".

"The Stalk" where Captain McNeill (with telescope) urges silence as the party is close to its quarry.

"The Death" with the stalker admiring the stag's fine antlers while Captain McNeill pours a celebratory dram.

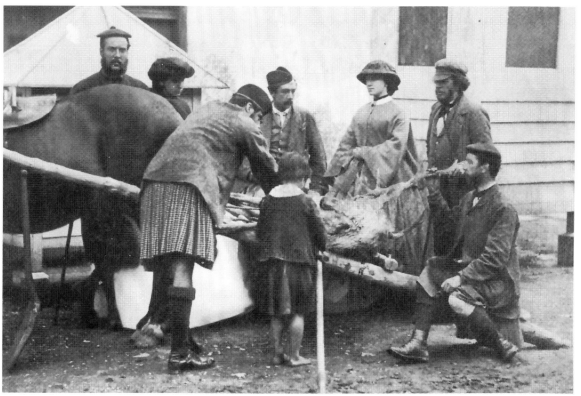

"The Return" is outside the game larder at the lodge. The stag has been brought down from the hill on a slype (sledge) drawn by a pony.

those we know now, while most of the lodges had been rebuilt and extended, very much as they are today.

1884/85 Season[37]

GROUND	GAMEKEEPER
The Duke's, West Hand	Donald Macbeath
	William Campbell
Sronphadruig	Hugh Macdonald
Dalnaspidal	James Gow
Dalnacardoch	John MacLachlan
Dalnamein	James Thompson
Clunes	John Dow
Glen Bruar	Peter Campbell
Kindrochet	James Stewart
Bohespic	John Cameron
Strathtummel	Alex Forbes
Loch Valligan	Thomas Ritchie
Glen Fernate	John McBeath
Fealar	Donald Lamont

Birds of prey were particularly vulnerable in the eighteenth century, as the following account, submitted by a keeper in 1753, of birds destroyed and payments made, shows:[38]

			Sterling £	s	d
Game Hawks	4 eggs	2 young	1		0
Merlin Hawks	5 eggs				6
Gleads [Kites]	4 eggs	2 young	1		6
Haddie [Hoodie] Crows	46 eggs	29 young	7		5
Ravens		3 young			6
Magpies	82 eggs	9 young	3		4½
To Frederick Crerar for a wild cat			5		0
			19		3½

A study of the Atholl game books reveals that almost anything that moved was shot and the total of each type of animal and bird killed in 1884/85 makes salutary reading:[39]

Stag	208	Brown Hare	865
Hind	130	White Hare	648
Fallow Deer (Dunkeld)	73	Rabbit	2,111
		Trapped Rabbit	7,467
Roe Deer	40	Fox	117
Grouse (brace)	7,475	Weasel	376
Black Grouse	238	Hoodie Crow	147
Ptarmigan	103	Hawk	137
Capercaillie	7	Peregrine Falcon	2
Partridge	993	Raven	15
Pheasant	766	Owl	21
Woodcock	60	Magpie	21
Snipe	125	Jay	46
Wild Fowl	87	Cat	159
Plover	50	Hedgehog	209
Wood Pigeon	18	Squirrel	70

Deer

Red deer are the largest animals hunted in Atholl and one of the noblest in appearance:

> It is an animal combining innocence with guile in a way which drew the best out of hounds and hunters to make the chase a physical as well as a mental exercise. Its solitary nature in the hunting season makes the selection of an individual stag a possibility.[40]

The old term for stag is "hart" and this appears in quoted extracts throughout the book, although it was falling out of general use by the early part of the twentieth century.

The fallow deer is half the size of the red deer and is no longer found in the Atholl deer forests north of the Pass of Killiecrankie. One of the largest herds in Scotland is to be found in the Tulliemet forest, south of Pitlochry.

The roe is the smallest of the native deer species, and at a quarter of the size of red, is "dainty and spare". It is much less numerous in the woodlands round Blair Castle than it used to be, so that numbers shot today are few.

Sandy McAra in 1856.

Donald Macbeath in 1856.

GAMEKEEPERS AND SPORTSMEN

Gamekeepers were put in charge of the running of the Atholl deer forests over three hundred years ago and one of the most prominent and the longest serving of them was John Crerar. He was born in 1750 at Ferniehaugh near Dunkeld, the second son of Alexander (Sandy) Crerar, who was fowler to the 2nd, 3rd and 4th Dukes of Atholl. In his early days Sandy lived at Warren House near Dunkeld and was paid £5 a year. Between 15 July and 18 August 1747, his account for "Gun Powder and Shote" was £1.10.0 Sterling and in 1757/58 he claimed the following wage and expenses:[1]

	Sterling		
	£	s	d
Wages Mart. 1757 to Mart. 1758	8	0	0
Servant Charles Robertson his wages	1	5	0
Our son	1	5	0
Maintenance of a firrett for a year preceeding Mart 1758	1	0	0
Lock for the bigg powder flask			8
Check brasshead to a lead bagg		2	0
	£11	12	8

This account was paid on 28 December 1758 by Major Harrison, private secretary to the 2nd Duke.

Sandy Crerar, father of John Crerar and Fowler to the 2nd, 3rd and 4th Dukes of Atholl, is on the far left of this family scene in 1780. John, 4th Duke, is to his right, with his oldest son, John, Marquis of Tullibardine. The old Blair Castle is in the background. (David Allen)

Frederick, the eldest son, was also employed as a gamekeeper on the Atholl estate and was very active in 1776, recruiting at the time of the American War of Independence, when he persuaded a number of local men to enlist. After this period he first became a postman in Dunkeld and later kept the inn which was near the cathedral. After it became a private residence, it was renamed St Adamnan's Cottage which was the home of the Dowager 6th Duchess Anne. It was pulled down around 1900, after her death.

John Crerar

John Crerar entered the service of the Atholl family as a gamekeeper in 1776 and remained with them until he died at the great age of ninety in 1840. He married Annie Stewart, who, on the death of her brother, James, in the West Indies in 1794, inherited his estate worth nearly £500. Its contents make strange reading nowadays:[2]

		£
10 Field Negroes at £75, this currency, each, is		825
Dall, whom he promised her freedom		75
Horses and cloths		60
		960
		£
Debts	2 Negroes	125
Debts		100
Funeral Charges		50	275
		£685

The money was in West Indian currency, of which the Sterling equivalent was £489. The names of his negroes were: James, Bob, George, Chelsea, Charles, Prince, Nancy, Sally, Mally, Betty and Dall.

John Crerar paid great attention both to the deer and other wildlife in the Atholl forests, which before his time had been largely neglected. His depth of knowledge and experience of his subject is clearly demonstrated in his paper *Observations upon a red deer forest and the method of keeping it*, which he wrote in the early part of the nineteenth century and a few extracts follow:[3]

STALKING
Look sharp if you see ptarmigan or moorfowls before you. Take care you do not startle these birds which will put them off with more fright than a sight of you would do at some distance. If you are lying near the deer for a shot and ptarmigans or moorfowl are between you and the deer and the eagle comes over your head, these birds will get away but the deer will not move. When a moorcock is startled he calls out and likewise his hen but not so loud and this sends the deer away. When the eagle appears the moorfowls are silent as they fly away and this will not disturb the deer.

FAWNS
A red deer is a wild and shy creature in this part of the world. Take hold of a fawn before it "takes to

"Death of a Hart in Glen Tilt" by Sir Edwin Landseer (1824-30)
Left to right: Charles Crerar (son of John Crerar) about to gralloch the deer; Donald McIntyre, keeper, Glen Tilt; the Hon George Murray, who became the 6th Duke in 1846; John, 4th Duke and John Crerar with his spyglass.

Donald Gow, an Atholl gamekeeper in 1856.

Jock Robertson, an Atholl gamekeeper in 1856.

Captain Alexander McDuff, estate factor from 1838 to 1865 and an Adjutant in the Atholl Highlanders.

Peter Fraser succeeded John Crerar as head keeper and held that position until 1847. By the time of this photograph in 1856 he was crippled with arthritis.

Peter Stewart, who took over from Donald Macbeath as head gamekeeper in 1905. (Hamish Paterson 1919)

William McAra, a gamekeeper, who as a young boy saw Queen Victoria in 1844. He was presented to Queen Mary when she visited Blair Castle in 1919 and again to King George V in 1921. (Hamish Paterson 1919)

Sandy Stewart, alias Alasdair Mor, gamekeeper and Pipe Major of the Atholl Highlanders (Hamish Paterson 1920)

Duncan Stewart, Atholl head gamekeeper in the early part of the 20th century. (Hamish Paterson 1919)

the foot", that is before it leaves the spot where it was born and stroke it down its back and ears for five minutes before putting a finger in its mouth. That fawn will then follow you home for at least seven miles or more.

DEER-HOUNDS
Another way is to let a greyhound dog chase a deer down to a burn where there are at least two greyhounds placed there. A person well skilled in this way of hunting must go with the first dog and another person must be at the burn to bring the deer down. This is the most difficult part as if the dog lets the deer run over the hill, the sport is over.

EAGLES
There are sixteen aires [eyries] in the forests of Atholl where I have seen the eagles build their nests. They build on a shelf of the rock not difficult to get at in sum places. Other rocks are smooth from bottom to top and there may be a spot somewhere in the smooth face where no one can get at it, as Carn Ree [Fealar]. In the south side of Glen Bruar there is a spot upon the top of a little rock or rather a large stone where the eagle used to build her nest. One might ride upon horseback to the nest as no wild beast or bird ever meddles with either the eagle or with her nest. The eagle cares very little where she builds only she takes care that she builds where there is a perpendicular of a good height underneath her. When she gets off the nest she will take wing with greater force. She has her eggs the first week of April and the first year she lays two eggs and has only one young, the other being rotten. Next year she has three eggs and two young, the third being rotten.

Golden Eagle.

She never has more than three eggs and every year are rots. They will build in the same place for years.

MOUNTAIN HARES
The mountain or white hare frequents the very highest tops of mountains in summer. They feed at night and in the daytime they sit near a large stone with a hole on one side and when the eagle comes in sight she bolts into the hole.

White or Mountain Hare.

BLACK COCK
The black cock is something like the hart who has his rutting time in October while the black cock is in April and May. The hart roars at the hinds and the blackcock has his ruling stance and shrieks at the hens.

A Black Cock lek near Trinafour.

2ND DUKE
When his Grace was young and horses a truble he always set out in the morning as soon as daylight. One morning going up Glen Tilt at the lower town, passing one of these towens, the road passing the door of one house a woman sat beside the door not

Eagles, hares and black cock are vividly described in John Crerar's paper, "Observations upon a red deer forest ..." (Paintings by Roger Lee)

five yards from the road, and a boy upon her knees. The woman was very bussie searching the boys head and catching so many and so bussily despatching her game that his Grace passed her unobserved. The man behind with the deer dogs making sum voice the woman looked up and seeing his Grace and followers, threw the boy on his back and ran into the house. His Grace turning round said for as early as we are in the morning, that woman has drawn blood before us and taken more lives than we shall do this day.

Game Licences

An Act was passed in the reign of George III, stating that:

> ... every person in Great Britain who shall use any dog, gun, net, other engine for the taking or destruction of game shall annually take out a certificate ... for any hare, pheasant, partridge, heathfowl, commonly called blackgame or grouse or any other game whatsoever ... without such certificate shall forfeit and pay twenty pounds.[4]

The inability to produce such a certificate and failure to give one's name and address, resulted in a fine of £50. If this fine was not paid, one or more Justices of the Peace presided over the case, with powers to "committ the offender to the common gaol or house of correction, there to remain for six months". John Crerar's certificate of 1815 was signed by William Lowndes, first commissioner of the tax office in Perth and a man described as having a "fractious and violent disposition". In 1820 game certificates were issued to the following people:[5] Duke of Atholl £3.14.6; Mr Graham (factor) £3.14.6; John Crerar £1.6.0; Charles Crerar £1.6.0; Donald McIntyre £1.6.0; George Ritchie £1.6.0, amounting to a total of £12.13.0.

John Crerar's regular reports to the 4th Duke at the start of the nineteenth century make fascinating reading. They clearly show that he had a discerning eye for everything around him and was an astute observer of wildlife in the deer forests. Here are a few examples:

26 February 1826

The other day there was a house cat wanting into the eagles cage. The eagle got hold of its head and pulled him in [and] did for the poor cat.[7]

9 April 1826

Since this fine weather the black cocks are making plenty of noise upon every hill around and plenty of pheasants both sides of the river.[8]

21 May 1826

The last week has been a very warm week indeed. The moon is full this afternoon with an eclipse at same time. Should think it would bring rain.[9]

Wages and Allowances

In addition to a basic wage, the estate paid for gamekeepers' work clothing and footwear and in 1827 this amounted to £68.14.0, made up thus:[6]

JOHN CRERAR, GAMEKEEPER

		£	s	d
Money wages		20	0	0
Meal, 6½ bolls 20/-		6	10	0
2 cows keeping £20 0 0				
Deduct dung 8 0 0				
12 0 0				
Add 4 bolls of potatoes in lieu of dung 1 12 0		13	12	0
2 suits of short grays at £4.10.0		9	0	0
1 suit of short green		4	10	0
1 suit of long green in 2 years £4.10.0 (1/2)		2	5	0
4 flannel jackets		1	8	0
3 pairs of hose		0	7	0
1 bonnet		0	3	6
2 pair of hill shoes		0	18	0
1 plaid in 2 years valued at £1.10.0 (1/2)		0	15	0
1 pair of mittens		0	1	6
1 pair of grey gaiters		0	10	0
4 pair of breeches valued at £1.0.0		4	0	0
1 pair of breeches in 2 years (1/2)		0	10	0
1 great coat in 4 years £1.4.0 (1/4)		0	6	0
1½ st. candles		0	18	0
House rent valued at		3	0	0
		£68	14	0

John Crerar's Music

Amongst his many other talents, John Crerar seems to have shown early signs of musical ability and he became a pupil of Niel Gow, who lived at Inver, near Dunkeld and in his time, the supreme exponent of Scottish fiddle music. The Atholl family, who were patrons of Niel Gow and took him to London, paid for these lessons. The many reels and airs he composed show he had a good idea of writing correct dance music and simple tunes. Titles mostly refer to the forests of which he was so fond, or are named after various members of the Atholl family. Of his earlier reels, "Forest Lodge", "The Duke of Atholl's Forest", "The Banks of the Garry" and "The Bridge of the Garry at Struan" were published in 1786. Other tunes composed by him include: "Craigie Barns", "The Bein-a-Glo Hunt", "Lady Emily Percy's Welcome to Scotland", "Lord James Murray's Wedding Day", "Hon George Murray's Strathspey", "Miss Charlotte Murray's Reel", "The Bridge of Dunkeld" and many more.[10]

Failing Health

By the 1820s, John Crerar's health was causing some anxiety as shown in reports:

12 March 1824 Fred Graham

John Crerar goes off tomorrow, and will leave Edinburgh for London on Monday morning, if he is allowed by the doctor he means to consult - as he says he cannot travel by sea, and is not quite sure whether he is fit for such a journey by land.[11]

23 December 1827 John Crerar

... my right eye continues still keeping darker than my other eye ... I rather think it is getting worse ...[12]

Oil portrait of John Crerar, gamekeeper, wildlife observer and Scottish dance music composer, born in 1750 and died 1840.
The painting is inscribed "... by Landseer, painted at Blair Atholl in 1824, Keeper John Crerar with pony". It was one of a number of preparatory
sketches which Landseer used in his large oil painting "Death of a Hart in Glen Tilt".
(Reproduced by permission of Perth & Kinross District Council, Museum & Art Gallery Dept., Scotland).

The house beside Polney Loch where John Crerar spent his final years until his death in1840.

24 February 1828

... The snow was so bright this last week that I could not travel out as it had such an effect on my eyes, though I had the preserves upon my eyes. When I came within doors I could hardly see anything for five minutes. The doctor was here two days ago and has a better opinion of the worst eye than he has of the one I see with ...[13]

6 April 1828

... my right eye I begin to see the light straight forward but cannot make out any objects except anything white about a yard from me.[14]

8 April 1829

Now that I can see a little round me I took a walk to see the new drive through Dunkeld. I went to see the new Palace. I got in among the work, and could not get my way out till I called of Charles [his son], who was with me. I may say I was the first who lost himself in the new Palace.[15]

John, 4th Duke of Atholl died in 1830 and left John Crerar an annuity of £25, which he enjoyed for a further ten years. To the end he kept up his keenness for the game of curling and on his ninetieth birthday, the Dunkeld Curling Club presented him with a silver quaich. Many a game did he watch from his cottage beside Polney Loch where he died at the great age of ninety. He was buried in Dowally churchyard where there is a table stone erected by Marjory, 4th Duchess of Atholl and his epitaph reads:

> John Crerar 1.3.1840 90 years
>
> Esteemed and respected for more than 50 years Constant and faithful attendant of John 4th Duke of Atholl in the sports of the forest the field and the stream

John Crerar's son, Charles, was born in 1798 and followed in his father's footsteps, becoming the Glen Tilt gamekeeper. His wages and allowances were £20 less than his father's, amounting in 1826/27 to £48.10.0 made up as follows:[16]

CHARLES CRERAR

	£	s	d
Money wages	12	0	0
1 suit of grays and 1 suit of green	9	0	0
Plaid at £1.10.0 (1/2)	0	15	0
Hill shoes	1	2	0
Bonnet	0	3	6
Mittens	0	1	6
House rent valued at £2	2	0	0
Board wages during the family's absence at the rate of 9/- per week which may be said to be per annum	23	8	0
	£48	10	0

For several years Charles had been thinking of leaving the Atholl estate. When his father retired as head keeper, he felt he had a better claim to it than anyone else but the job was given to Peter Fraser, while Charles was offered the post of keeper in the Grouse Department . He declined this but in 1834 the leases of the Tilt and Beinn a' Ghlo forests were taken up by the Duke of Buccleuch who offered Charles the position of being his head gamekeeper, because of his intimate knowledge of the ground. When this new appointment was offered Charles immediately accepted, as it offered better wages and conditions.

When he handed in his notice, angry words passed between him and the Duke who was obviously piqued that anyone should want to leave his employ. Before Charles departed, he arranged to sell off his household possessions in his house in Glen Tilt and the sale was advertised at the Blair Atholl church. Just before the sale he received a message from the castle forbidding this and although he complained in person to the Duke, it was to no avail. He was therefore forced to transport everything down to Blair Atholl and "sell there at a considerable loss".[17]

Peter Fraser

Peter Fraser, who was born in 1789, spent all his life in Glen Tilt, living first at Clachglas. He was appointed head keeper in 1830 on the retirement of John Crerar, holding this position until he retired through ill health in 1847. He was described as "a clever fellow with great strength and good wind. A regular descendant of servitude to the House of Atholl and an inhabitant of the country ..."[18]

The McAra Family

Sandy McAra, son of John McAra, shepherd in Ach Mhairc Bhig, in Glen Tilt, was born in 1810. He married Jean, one of the castle dairymaids who was employed at the time of Lord Glenlyon's marriage in 1839 to Anne Home Drummond, the 6th Duchess. In her account of her arrival at Blair Castle as a new bride she recorded that "At the front door of the castle, as it was considered unlucky for a bride to walk into her new home, I was lifted over the threshold by some of the Atholemen, while an oatcake was broken over my head by aid of a string pulled by Jean, the Dairymaid, afterwards wife of Sandy McAra ..."[19]

Sandy became Lord Glenyon's footman in the 1830s and was appointed head keeper in 1847 in place of Peter Fraser, but gave up in 1864 to take charge of the deer parks. He retired completely in 1871, becoming the first tenant of the Porter's Lodge at the main entrance to the castle and died in 1888. His older brother, John (Jock), who was born in 1800 and died in 1880, was also an Atholl keeper and in 1830 was paid as follows:[20]

	£	s	d
Wages	10	10	0
Milk money whilst at Ben y Glo	1	8	0
Meal	5	11	6
	17	9	6

Willie McAra was only a young boy when Queen Victoria stayed at Blair Castle in 1844 and when Queen Mary visited the area in 1919 he was introduced to her, as he alone remembered that earlier royal visit. Likewise when George V stopped for lunch at the castle on his way to Balmoral in 1921, Willie was presented to him as well.[21]

Donald Macbeath

Donald Macbeath, Glen Tilt's most famous son, was born in 1831. He was described as being a well-built man, 5 feet 10 inches in height, with blue eyes, a Roman nose, dark brown hair and whiskers. He took snuff, wore a coat of coloured squares with grey trousers which had two white stripes on the inside of each leg.[22] Such was his strength that when a wounded deer was held at bay in the Tilt, he waded in, killed it and single-handed dragged it across the river.

At the age of twenty he enlisted in the Scots Fusilier Guards and embarked three years later for the Crimea where he served with great distinction. He returned to Atholl after the war when he took over from Sandy McAra as head keeper in 1864. His prowess as brigade sharpshooter in the Crimea rapidly became evident in his shooting exploits. Between November 1866 and March the following year he personally shot over a hundred hinds and the next October accounted for fourteen stags.

The East Lodge, gateway to Glen Tilt, was built in 1884 when Donald became its first occupant. He was sergeant major in the Atholl Highlanders and retired from work in 1905, his place being taken by Peter Stewart, son of John Stewart, another Atholl hillman. Donald fell ill in February 1911 through kidney failure and died at the end of the month. The 7th Duke recorded

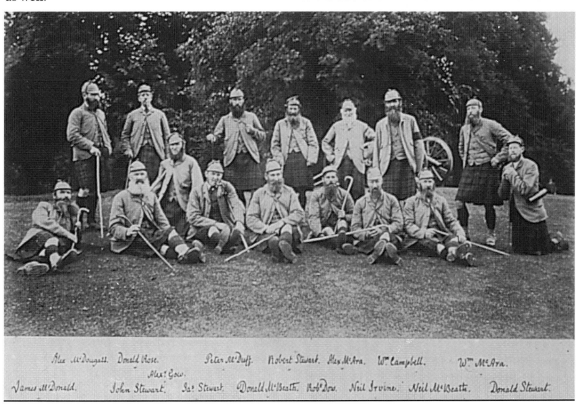

Alex McDougall. Donald Rose. Peter McDuff. Robert Stewart. Alex McAra. Wm Campbell. Wm McAra.
Alext Gow.
James McDonald. John Stewart. Jas Stewart. Donald McBeath. Rob Dow. Neil Irvine. Neil McBeath. Donald Stewart.

Hillmen and keepers in the castle grounds in 1886.

his passing in the Atholl Highlanders Record Book:

> Sergeant Major Macbeath, a representative of one of the Glen Tilt families of former days, and one of the finest looking men who ever joined the Atholl Highlanders, after a short service in the 92nd Highlanders, entered the Atholl Highlanders in 1849 and was promoted to sergeant the following year. In 1852 he enlisted in the Scots Fusilier Guards and served through the whole of the Crimean War without a day's illness. He was appointed a sergeant and received the Crimean Medal with 4 clasps, the Turkish Medal and the Distinguished Conduct Medal. On the peace in 1856 he took his discharge and rejoined the Atholl Highlanders as Sergeant Major which rank he held till his death. He was the father of the regiment with a service of 58 years.[23]

The following poem could be his fitting epitaph:

The Old Stalker

His hair was all a badger grey,
His eyes were full of break-o'-day,
His voice was like the winds that stray
  In a high corrie.
Six feet his height; his years four score;
His shoulders filled his cottage door;
His strength - they called him Iain Mor -
  Was the glen's glory.

J. B. Salmond

SPORTSMEN

Hundreds of sportsmen, some famous and many others not so, have leased the Atholl shooting lodges and moorlands over the past 150 years but space limitations enable only three to be covered in this section.

William Scrope

William Scrope was one of the leading sportsmen of the Victorian era and a great authority on the subject. He first appeared on the Atholl scene in 1822, having obtained a glowing reference from the novelist, Sir Walter Scott, enabling him to rent Bruar Lodge. By this time, he was over fifty and he stalked for only ten years in Atholl before reluctantly falling back on less energetic field sports like fishing.

His most famous book *The Art of Deer Stalking* was first published in 1837 and has been reprinted several times since. Its dedication to the 4th Duchess of Atholl, the Hon. Marjory Forbes, showed how keenly he missed the Atholl deer forests:

> Years have passed over the exciting amusement which they treat of, but the glories of the Highland landscape, though faded from my view, are dear to my remembrance and I look back, as from out of a cheerless glen, upon those distant and sunny scenes of my life. Yes the pleasures of my mountain sport are indeed at an end; but my deep gratitude towards those, through whose kindness and hospitality I enjoyed both that sport, and the delightful society by which it was varied has not passed away with the fleeting hours, but has rather been strengthened by time and circumstance.

Scrope was a classical scholar at Eton and also an accomplished landscape artist. In 1824 John Crerar received a note from the estate factor, informing him that "Mr Landseer, the celebrated painter of animals is to visit Blair to obtain information regarding red deer and to get a glimpse of the great herds in Glen Tilt".[24]

Landseer

Sir Edwin Landseer spent ten days studying Glen Tilt and thereafter was a guest of William Scrope at Bruar Lodge, where he was introduced to the adjacent hills and became a keen stalker. He repeated his visits in 1825 and 1826 during which time he executed portraits of several hill men and subsequently painted the well-known picture "Death of a Hart in Glen Tilt". For the illustrations in his deer-stalking book, Scrope first drew the landscape backgrounds and then invited friends like Charles and Edwin Landseer to complete the deer and dog scenes.

A stalking scene from "The Art of Deer Stalking" in which William Scrope drew the background and one of the Landseer brothers added in the figures.

Year after year Scrope returned to Bruar Lodge until he became part of the scenery, with the Duke appointing him as a sort of honorary head gamekeeper and he found himself almost in complete control of a vast tract of moorland. From Bruar he kept Blair Castle supplied with grouse and venison. His favourite method of stalking was to set out with three or four retainers, one carrying the rifles, one holding the deer-hounds on a leash and the others to carry out flanking movements. The flankers would suddenly appear on a distant ridge and drive the deer in the direction where Scrope was waiting.

In some respects his stalking was similar to modern techniques and even if he did not invent them, he was certainly the first to record the process in detail. He was taken into the hearts of the Atholl people and soon formed a close and affectionate relationship with those stalkers like

John Crerar and Peter Fraser, humorously referring to himself as "Tortoise" in his book.

Walter Winans

Walter Winans, American millionaire and sportsman, who was a great exponent of deer driving and rented Forest Lodge for a season.

Walter Winans, the great American philosopher, poet, soldier, explorer, artist and millionaire, rented most of the Atholl deer forest in 1871, basing himself at Forest Lodge. By the early 1880s he held shooting rights over vast areas of Scotland, covering something like 200,000 acres.

Reporting on his sporting activities after his death, The *Shooting Times* editor wrote:

> Mr Winan's Deer Forests
> There is nothing in all forest history to compare with the paying of £18,000 a year of rental for deer forests, a performance which the late Mr Walter Winans kept up for many years, even after he stopped firing a shot or coming up North. He kept a big army of beaters and keepers, and we are probably not far from the mark in putting down his expenditure on the forests as exceeding quarter of a milllion pounds during the period when they were silent ... his area stretched from the North Sea to the Atlantic and embraced 12 separate lets.[25]

Winans broke the unwritten rules of the Victorian sporting code by indulging in deer driving which he organised on a gigantic scale. He was brilliant with a rifle and frequently killed a galloping stag at a distance of two hundred yards. This was seen as a remarkable feat as the ordinary shooter felt he did well if he shot a stationary stag at 100 yards. His drives were organised with the thoroughness of a military operation and he was known to employ as many as forty men at a time. It was probably jealousy that goaded many of his critics into print, as they were envious of his prowess and the immense amount of sport he enjoyed. He defended the practice of deer driving vigorously in print:

> This is an unfortunate combination of words to describe moving deer towards the shooters. It has led to the "driving deer into a narrow place where they have no escape" style of abusing those who indulge in this form of sport. If the writers of such nonsense themselves tried to drive deer, they would find how impossible it is. Deer will not be driven; if they think they are being forced, they will break back, however thick the beaters are ...[26]

His fanatical enthusiasm and success was reminiscent of the great tinchels of medieval

Walter Winans in Glen Tilt, setting out for a day's sport in the hills.

days when hundreds of deer were slaughtered. He was a great authority on every aspect of the sport and much of this is recorded in the several books he wrote on the subject. *The Sporting Rifle* published in 1908, showed plans of two ideal drives and one such manoeuvre he recalled, yielded no fewer than thirty one stags. Other books on the subject of firearms included *Practical Rifle Shooting, The Art of Revolver Shooting* and *Hints on Revolver Shooting.* He also contributed regularly to magazines and newspapers, and wrote to *The Shooting Times* in 1915, as follows:

> Proportion of Royals
> I was struck by the small proportion of Royal Stags (12 points or more) which I have. They work out at a fraction under one Royal to every 29 stags I shot. My list to date is: Two Imperials, 18 points; two of 17 points, three of 15 points; two of 14 points; five of 13 points; 18 of twelve points.[27]

Towards the end of his life, Walter Winans presented Purdeys, the world-famous gunsmiths, with a folio of his drawings of stag shooting in the Highlands and also two signed bronzes of American cowboys sculpted by himself.

Horatio Ross

Captain Horatio Ross from Montrose, the twenty-seven year old godson of Admiral Nelson and hence his name, rented Fealar Lodge in 1828. This was to enable him to train himself for a grand shooting match he had set up on 1

Partridge in winter. (Roger Lee) Partridges were the subject of a wager by Horatio Ross.

November that year against a Colonel Anson. A large sum of money was staked on the contest in which the two men walked all day, on heathland at Mildenhall, Suffolk, shooting as many partridges as possible without the use of dogs. Ross's vigorous preparations paid off, as by the end of the contest, when the Colonel could walk no more, Ross discovered he was one bird ahead.

Fealar Lodge was advertised to let every year for the shooting season and space was taken in the *Edinburgh Courant*, the *Perthshire Advertiser* and the *General Advertiser* in April 1828, with London advertising also being considered.[28] Horatio Ross answered one of these advertisements and on receipt of the details and price, complained that for a rent of £262, he should be entitled to more ground to make the terms more compatible with those for the previous tenant, Sir David Moncreiff. "I am happy to give £300 on these revised conditions and spare no expense in protecting both the red deer and grouse", he wrote.[29]

The Duke's reply was that the terms were identical to those offered to the previous tenant and he declined to increase the area on offer, or indeed to grant a lease for more than a year at a time. Within a few days Ross tried again, offering to relinquish part of the south side of the Fealar ground "which the Duke wished to preserve", in exchange for a similar area of ground on the south side of the Tarf Water. A note in the Duke's hand indicates that permission to shoot there was also refused.[30]

Horatio Ross's bag for the season was 85 deer, 2,080 grouse, 152 ptarmigan, 9 wildfowl, 16 snipe and 17 hares. According to Scrope he had disregarded his quotas and overshot everything, especially grouse, where his allowance was 1,080 birds. It was said that he could not shoot an individual deer and overcame this handicap by firing into the herd, in the hope of killing one of them. The estate maintained that to achieve these huge totals, "it is quite evident that the forest was driven in the night". The Duke commented that "he proved to be a very troublesome tenant and also shot the ground very hard". His lease was not renewed for the following season despite the fact that he offered an additional £100 in rent.[31]

POACHING AND POACHERS

There is no mention of deer poachers in the chronicles of Scottish law until the twelfth century when an Act of Parliament was passed against them. If a forester found a stranger who had wandered into his forest, it was his duty to put him on the "nearest common way and then sall suffer him to passe away without anie trouble". If the trespasser became a regular offender, he was to be arrested, with his captor being allowed to remove his outer coat, all his money and then detain him. By 1567 the laws had become much more severe, so that anyone caught killing deer, who had no goods to forfeit, was sentenced to forty days imprisonment for a first offence, and if caught again, lost his right hand. "Hanging to the death" was the ultimate penalty for third time offenders.[1]

Because of their vastness and remoteness the Atholl forests provided great opportunities for poachers as shown in a document dated 2 May 1704 headed:

Abuses Committed in His Grace's Fforests of Atholl

It is informed that James Bane Robertsone and Lauchlan McPhearson, fforesters and indwellers in Dalmunzie in the country of Glenshee did make an constant trade of killing His Grace's deer summer last, being anno 1703 in the forrest of Ffreechrombie [Seven Shielings] whereof the said Lauchlan was forester, and did dispose of several of the said deer to low-country Lairds and Gentlemen, and particularly to the people of Marre, viz Lauchlan and John McIntoshes who made same fled from Glen Tilt and now reside in the braes of Marr and live all summer by killing deer in both fforests.[2]

Poaching on the Increase

By the 1750s the Atholl estate was becoming increasingly alarmed at the growing incidence of poaching, with the Lord Advocate observing that because of the extensive nature of the forests owned by the Duke, it was difficult to arrest

A group of Atholl hillmen in Blair Castle grounds in 1868.

Duncan Macdonald and Peter MacGregor, hillmen, in 1856.

Jock McAra, Keeper, in 1856.

offenders and take them to court. However, the Duke was anxious to start proceedings against anyone caught, despite the fact that leading members of the legal profession stressed the problems that the old laws were vague regarding killing deer especially in forests belonging to people like the Duke of Atholl. They declared that anyone shooting deer without permission was committing an offence but without proof it would appear "too trifling for a trial before the Court of Justiciary that the bringing of it would raise an clamour which might be easely improved to mislead a jury". They recommended therefore that one or two of the regular offenders be prosecuted before a sheriff as "a trespass against common law", thus dispensing with a jury.[3]

Plans were drawn up to prosecute known offenders and as a first step, advertisements were placed in newspapers warning of likely penalties. These were to be "modest and detrimmed" (determined) while keepers were instructed to warn known offenders and tenants told to take care with their dogs and swine.

Notable Poachers

About the year 1750 one noted poacher was caught and brought before the Duke. He claimed his weapons consisted of only a bow and arrow with which he was expert. The Duke did not believe him, and pointing out a stag, ordered him to shoot it in the eye and thus escape punishment. The archer gave a peculiar whistle at which the stag promptly turned round and the arrow duly found its mark.[4]

In 1783 the Duke called together his three senior gamekeepers, John Crerar, James Moon

and Peter Robertson, promising a handsome reward to the one who killed the fattest stag within two days, as it was to be sent off as a present to George III. Crerar and Moon set off the following morning, each accompanied by a hillman and pony, as if on a normal expedition. However, the third keeper, Peter Robertson, travelled north to the forest of Gaick, where he knew there was a tame stag of exceptional size. This stag lived luxuriously all summer, grazing fresh pasture and in winter was housed in a barn, living off oats, barley and pease, so that by the time he was five he had reached extraordinary dimensions. After plying the two shepherds guarding the stag with far too much whisky for their own good, Peter Robertson made off with it, and when out of rifle shot, dispatched the animal and brought it back to Blair Castle, where he was the easy winner of the prize.[5]

Niel and then Nathaniel Gow's cottage in Inver, near Dunkeld around 1900.

John and Donald Stewart, a piper, (they were not related) were caught in 1810 with the carcase of a hind in their house and were imprisoned. John's brother, Robert, was the constable in charge of them at the jail and proceeded to let them escape, so that he in turn was locked up in his own jail, while the other two were not to be found. The factor was instructed to send a search party after them, as it was felt there was a possibility of catching them on a Sunday morning, since they would most likely be unaware that a "common warrant" operated even on the Sabbath day.[6]

Two years later there was a poaching incident involving a man called Armstrong, accused of killing a roe deer. The Duke was asked to deal leniently with him and clemency was recommended. It was suggested he should beg forgiveness from the Duke, pay all expenses incurred and donate £50 to the poor of Blair Atholl. This message was to be communicated to Armstrong by his father-in-law, Nathaniel Gow, one of the four children of the famous Scots fiddler, Niel Gow. Nathaniel himself was a master of the violin, credited by some as even greater an exponent than his father. Perhaps this connection explains the efforts made to "go easy" on the poacher.

John Crerar was always concerned with checking poaching activities and was able to give the following favourable report to the Duke on 5 February 1817:

> ... there has been no complaints of potchers of the forest as there has been no particular order for killing any game for London.[7]

Years later he was summoned to court in unusual circumstances as is recorded in his report dated 2 April 1826:

> Mr Graham told me sum days ago that tomorrow was a justice court day and the potcher that Charles [Crerar] and Fraser seed above Blackies was to be at the court and that I should bring the potcher's dog into Court to see if the dog would know the potcher. If so, the Justice might form the judgment against him the better ... Since this fine weather the Black Cocks are making plenty of noise upon every hill round and plenty of pheasants both sides of the river.[8]

Captain Alexander Macduff, the factor, was constantly urging his keepers to be on the look-out for poachers and was able to report that John, Kinaldy and John Robertson caught William Mackenzie from Knappaig with six hares in his possession. To ensure his appearance in court to give evidence, Macduff had kept the double-barrelled shotgun that Mackenzie had with him when caught.[9]

In 1830 two Macdonald brothers were caught poaching deer and escorted to Perth by Charles McGregor, the ground officer, where they were questioned by the sheriff. They admitted that part of a deer had indeed been found in their father's house but insisted it had not been taken from any of the Duke's deer forests. Since they refused to say where it had come from, they were therefore committed to prison to await further examination. George Condie, the Duke's Perth law agent admitted there was no evidence that they had been seen carrying arms at night for the purpose of poaching and indicated that it would

Glen More and Carn an Righ, the mountain near Fealar, where Lonavey hid his gun in a cave.

be difficult to obtain a conviction under the Act of George IV, interpreting it as follows: "Deer in their natural state were held to be wild animals and could not be stolen unless from a park in which they were confined, when they became private property".[10]

Thomas Duncan, the procurator fiscal, told Condie he was in no doubt about the guilt of the two brothers, especially after the evidence of a member of the McAra family. This seemed to be further strengthened when their father absconded on being told to report to Blair to be interviewed. "Unfortunately there is almost no legal evidence upon which to venture a prosecution", the fiscal observed.

Lonavey

Some three hundred years ago a famous poacher called Lonavey (Mackeracher) hunted freely through the Atholl forests. Although he had only one hand, he was a superb rifle shot, and having helped the Atholl men win a shooting competition against the English, the Earl of the time granted him the freedom to shoot deer on his land. All this changed when a new Earl succeeded to the title and lands of Atholl and Lonavey was duly apprehended and imprisoned, but not before he had hidden his famous gun in a cave, near Carn an Righ, in the Fealar forest.

Just before he died, he confided to a fellow inmate in Perth prison, the whereabouts of his concealed gun. To preserve his gun, Lonavey had smeared it with deer tallow and positioned it in such a way, that on one day a year, the sun's rays would shine on it. Many years later, another famous poacher, John Farquharson, shot a stag on Carn an Righ and was on the point of gralloching it, when three keepers came into view. He quickly concealed himself in a cave he stumbled on by chance and when his eyes became accustomed to the gloom, he discovered the remains of the legendary Lonavey gun.[11]

John Farquharson was born in the 1830s at Daldhu in Glenfernate and from an early age his ambition was to become a gamekeeper. He was a man of medium height, with clear, keen grey eyes and his first post was with Lord Abercromby. He became a champion rifle shot and invented the "Farquarson position" in which the marksman fired his rifle lying flat on his back, with his left arm passed round his head to his right shoulder and the rifle laid across his body. Another invention of his is recorded for 1870, when he took out a patent on a new form of cartridge extractor. The restrictions and expectations of his employers frustrated Farquharson and his longing for the freedom and adventure of the hills became too strong, resulting in him turning poacher and outwitting his former colleagues and fellow keepers.

Another famous poacher was Alexander Davidson, who was born in 1792 near Crathie on Deeside and he started his working life as a keeper with Lord Kennedy who had rented the Fealar deer forest. Davidson did not remain long, for, as he said, "Sooner than be in any way a flunkey, I'd rather go and beg". He was disgusted because his employer totally disregarded the Sabbath and went out shooting as usual on that day. He refused to accompany him and was outraged by the fast and immoral life-style that Lord Kennedy and his friends led. One day when they were passing Blair Castle, Kennedy had wagered Davidson, in jest, that he would give him £500 if he shot the Duke. "Though Your Lordship would give me £5,000 I would not do it, for I have a soul to be saved as well as Your Lordship's", he replied.[12] Horatio Ross said of Kennedy: "He was a spoilt child all his life".

Lord Kennedy's Wager

Although he was extremely wealthy, Lord Kennedy frittered away most of his (and his wife's) fortune through high living and making extravagant wagers. *The Romance of Poaching in the Highlands* by W. McCombie Smith, records an unusual one which took place in 1820:

> ... Mr Innes of Durris and Mr Davidson of Balnagask, backed Davidson, against Lord Kennedy and Mr Farquharson of Finzean, who had wagered £50 that Davidson would not run naked from Barclay Street, Stonehaven to the gate of Inchmarlo in a given time. Lord Kennedy and Finzean thought Davidson's feet would give way, but to still further insure their winnings, they ignobly hired a posse of wives, armed with stones, their leader, a Mrs Duncan having also a large knotty stick, to waylay Davidson at the Bridge of Banchory and prevent him crossing. When Davidson came in sight of the bridge and saw the party of Amazons, he rested a minute or two to regain his wind, and then charged down on them, and so wild was his appearance, and so terrific the speed with which he bounded into their midst, that their missiles fell harmlessly wide of their mark, and he passed the bridge unscathed, leaving discomfited wives raging shrilly in the rear. He reached Inchmarlo well within time, and got the £50.

There was little scruple amongst men like John Farquharson in taking deer from the Atholl forests because many people still believed that it had always been a royal forest and that the Earls and Dukes were merely the King's head keepers who were not affected by their activities, as the deer belonged to the King. Another source of resentment was that in a poor country, where food was often scarce, so much meat was reserved for the nobility, who needed it much less than anyone else.

FEALAR FOREST

Fealar (Benechrombie) 009 800 is the most remote of the Atholl deer forests and covers 12,500 acres, marching with Mar forest to the north and Glenfernate to the south. It was described in the 1920s by Alexander McConnachie in his book, *Deer and Deer Forests of Scotland*, in the following way:

> The pasture is excellent, there being few rocks, but many deep little glens which afford both food and shelter. The limit is sixty stags. The bag of grouse is very heavy, 1000 brace; other game includes snipe, duck, black game, ptarmigan and hares. There is much good trout fishing, besides an occasional salmon. Thus in September 1905 Mr Knox Brown (a guest of the tenant) killed three stags in the morning, caught a salmon in the Tilt in the afternoon, and shot a grouse immediately thereafter. The good feeding in Fealar attracts many deer; it has been estimated that about a thousand hinds remain all the year round. Both eagles and ravens nest within the forest.

Early Gamekeepers

John Stewart was given charge of Fealar forest in 1722 with "an allowance of twelve pounds Sterling yearly in name of salary or Forrester Fee with five guineas of wages yearly to his servant, stalker or assistant".[1] Ten years later he was issued with the following instructions which gave:

> ... full power to the said John Stewart and his servants or assistants to take care of and preserve the said forest by seizing and ingathering all bestial found therein not privileged to or tollerated by us the said John Duke of Atholl. As also to

Over a thousand brace of grouse were shot in a season in the Fealar forest in the 1920s. (Roger Lee)

> apprehend every person whom they find with dogs or guns in the said Forest of Benechrombie and carry them before the nearest Sheriff, Stewart or Justice of the Peace to be secured until they answer as accords the terms of the Act of 1685.[2]

The reason for impounding straying or trespassing beasts was that Fealar had been let out for shooting purposes to Donald Stewart who was given a "new tack [lease] for nynteen years after Whit. 1732".

Extensive Grazing

At this time the Fealar pasture was being extensively grazed during the summer months. Unlike other grazing grounds, which were let out to Atholl tenants, Fealar's grazing was leased to tenants outwith the area. In an account for 1758 it was shown that 313 head of cattle, belonging to twenty nine different owners, grazed at Fealar for a total cost of £79 Sterling. Grass money was paid at 5 shillings per head, unless there were more than twenty in the herd, when a discount of one free beast operated. Five herdsmen were employed to look after

Highland cattle at Loch Moraig. (Roger Lee)

ATHOLL DEER FORESTS
FEALAR • SEVEN SHIELINGS • LUDE • GLENFERNATE • TARF • TILT • BEINN A' GHLO

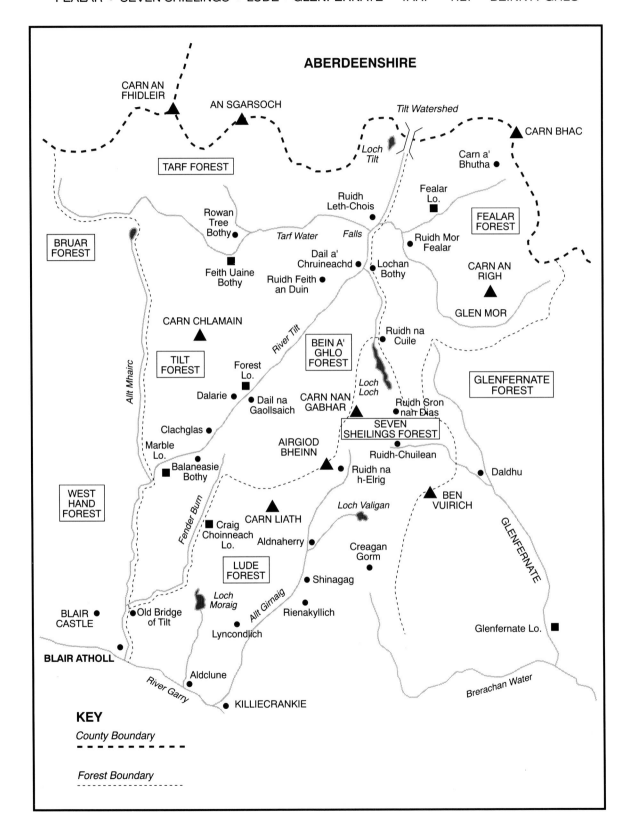

ABERDEENSHIRE

CARN AN FHIDLEIR

AN SGARSOCH

Tilt Watershed

CARN BHAC

Loch Tilt

TARF FOREST

Carn a' Bhutha

Fealar Lo.

FEALAR FOREST

Ruidh Leth-Chois

BRUAR FOREST

Rowan Tree Bothy

Tarf Water   *Falls*

Ruidh Mor Fealar

Dail a' Chruineachd

Lochan Bothy

CARN AN RIGH

Feith Uaine Bothy

Ruidh Feith an Duin

GLEN MOR

CARN CHLAMAIN

River Tilt

Ruidh na Cuile

TILT FOREST

Forest Lo.

BEIN A' GHLO FOREST

GLENFERNATE FOREST

Dalarie

Dail na Gaollsaich

CARN NAN GABHAR

Loch Loch

Ruidh Sron nan Dias

Allt Mhairc

Clachglas

SEVEN SHEILINGS FOREST

Marble Lo.

AIRGIOD BHEINN

Ruidh-Chuilean

Daldhu

Balaneasie Bothy

Ruidh na h-Elrig

WEST HAND FOREST

BEN VUIRICH

Loch Valigan

GLENFERNATE

CARN LIATH

Fender Burn

Craig Choinneach Lo.

Aldnaherry

Creagan Gorm

LUDE FOREST

Shinagag

Allt Girnaig

Loch Moraig

Rienakyllich

BLAIR CASTLE

Old Bridge of Tilt

Glenfernate Lo.

Lyncondlich

BLAIR ATHOLL

Aldclune

River Garry

Brerachan Water

KILLIECRANKIE

KEY

County Boundary

- - - - - - - -

Forest Boundary

- - - - - - - - - - - - - -

the animals and they were; John McLarin, wages £1.10.0 Sterling; John Forbes, Kenneth Mackenzie, John Cameron and Thomas Mackenzie, who were all paid £1.

The previous year had been more profitable as is shown in a Memorandum of 23 August "concerning the graseing of Fealar":

	Sterling		
	£	s	d
200 lowland oxen at 5 sh. each	50	0	0
123 herd of yeld cattle belonging to Lady Fintry at 5 sh. each	30	15	0
10 milk cows at 5 sh. each	2	10	0
200 wedders [sheep]	10	0	0
8 mares and foalls, 4 Highland mares, foalls	3	0	0
100 goats, 40 ewes and lambs	5	0	0
Nota: Besides the above, the herds have about a hundred head of cattle that Lady Fintry knows nothing of.	20	0	0
	£121	5	0

It is informed that it will fatten 400 oxen as well as could be desired and Glenmore reserved for the deer.[3]

This manuscript shows the extent of the Fealar pasture, capable of fattening nearly 750 livestock, outside that part of the forest set aside for deer. This was called Glen More, a steep-sided glen of some eight miles which passes round the south side of **Carn an Righ** (King's Cairn) 029 772, a 3,344 feet mountain, traditionally named after King Malcolm who often hunted there.

Horatio Ross was not the only Fealar tenant to cause problems to the Atholl estate, as in 1761 the Duke had cause to write to Lord Kinnaird to inform him that he:

> ... makes a very bad use of the warrant you have for leave to kill moorfowles upon the bounds of Glenmore, by haveing several others in company with you with Dogs, guns, and nets, Destroying the game. This will oblidge me to withdraw the warrant I gave you on 24th January 1759.[4]

The party in question consisted of Mr Menzies of Woodend, Mr Stewart of Gourdie and Mr Freebairne, the gauger (excise man) from Kirkmichael, whom the Duke threatened to report to his superior, as he spent too much time absent from his work. He decided to prosecute the others as they did not have game licences and "are not even qualified to carry a gun".

Fealar Lodge

There is very little recorded information about the lodge in the eighteenth century. Forty five loads of peat at 3d a load were delivered to the "House of Feath-Larie" in 1771 by the following: Donald Forbes in Achgoual, 23 loads; Patrick Stewart in Toidhnacoile, Alex Stewart in Dalnagoilsich, Donald Stewart in Aldandouth, Alex Stewart in Pitanasie, 4 loads each; Robert Stewart in Dalvorist, Alex Machbea and Donald Stewart in Clachglas, 2 loads each.

James Robertson was paid £2.10.0 Sterling for building the sheep fank in 1791 and two years

A clipping scene at Fealar in 1984 when nearly 600 ewes and hoggs were pastured.

later, John Forbes received £3.16.0 for thatching "the old house at Fealair". By 1801 the lodge was in a bad state of repair and the factor reported that "... the house is much destroyed by idle people who have broken open the doors and windows and stole most of the locks." Repairs were quickly put in hand and the lodge enlarged, as described in the factor's report:

> 18 June 1801
> I was at Felear yesterday, this dry season suits it. The pasture is remarkably good, the cattle and sheep are in fine order. I have the masons and carpenters at Felear house, it is a very difficult business to get the materials conveyed to it. Felear will be excellent shooting quarters this season. Great plenty of game and several of the broods are now flying and will be very strong by the twelfth of August.[5]

After the lodge had been rebuilt, it contained a dining room, drawing room, five bedrooms, kitchen, servants' hall, butler's room and servants' apartments. Lord Kennedy was an early tenant in the enlarged lodge and after inspecting it, was "well satisfied with everything". He did however, complain about the dog kennel, which measured 18 feet by 8 feet and wished this to be double the size and enclosed with railings "for airing the dogs". Both he and his fellow sportsman, Mr Skene, moved in for the 1821 season.

Another Wager

Lord Kennedy's wager involving Alexander Davidson in 1820 was surpassed by him two years later and an account of it, which was played for very high stakes, appeared in *The Times* for 31 August 1822:

> The decision of Lord Kennedy's great match for 2000 guineas took place on Monday, the 12th of August. His lordship had taken 40 to 1, in fifties, that he would, on day 1 of season 1822, from 12 o' clock of one night to 12 o' clock the following night, kill 40 brace of grouse, on his shooting farm at Fealar, at the head of Aberdeenshire; and afterwards ride to his seat at Dunnottar and back to Fealar, a distance of 140 miles.

> Exactly at 12 o' clock on Sunday night, three watches were set together, and put into a box by the umpires. At four in the morning Lord Kennedy commenced shooting, attended by a great body of Highlanders, drawn together from curiosity. A great deal of rain had fallen in the night, which made the hills very wet, and the birds wild. The first bird was killed at a quarter after four, and the whole 40 brace in four hours and 41 minutes. After shifting his wet clothes and taking some refreshment, he mounted his horse and started for Dunnottar, where he arrived at 2 o' clock, having rode the 70 miles in four and a half hours.

> He remained about an hour there and got back to Fealar four minutes before eight o' clock at night, performing the 140 miles in 10 hours and 26

Party at Fealar Lodge around 1900.

Fealar Lodge showing the keeper's cottage to the rear and the annexe in the foreground, built in 1911 to accommodate "two gentlemen and their servants".

Remains of the Lochain Bothy (Fealar Forest) with Glen Loch as a backdrop.

Two Highland ponies, "Kitty " and "Steelie", fording the Tilt after a day's stalk in 1850. (William Evans)

A shooting party returning to Blair Castle along the "Upper Avenue" in 1846. (William Evans)

The 6th Duke of Atholl in 1856 with his terrier "Tommy".

minutes. The whole was done, shooting, riding etc., in 15 hours and 56 minutes. He returned to Castletown that night, a distance of 14 miles by 10 o' clock, making the whole distance on horseback 154 miles.

His Lordship did not appear fatigued. Everything was against him; the grouse are uncommon strong and forward this season; the road is anything but good - the first four miles a mere mountain sheep track, and the remainder very hard and stony, with numerous short, sharp hills.

Within three years repairs to the lodge were necessary, as it had been left in a "very dilapidated state" by Mr Skene, who was sent a bill for the damage. The new tenant, Sir David Moncreiffe, asked for the rooms to be painted in a "blue water colouring" and for new grates for the dining room and two of the bedrooms. He also requested forms for the hall and small benches for the kennel.

Up to this time, the only way to approach Fealar was from Glen Tilt. About half a mile beyond the Falls of Tarf, a track can be seen, zig-zagging up the slope to the east, at the confluence of the two rivers that serve to form the Tilt, Allt Garbh Buidhe and Allt Feith Lair, where there is a ford. From here it is two miles across the tops of the hills to the lodge. Sir David wanted to change this and offered to widen and extend the bridle path made up Glenfernate in 1820, at his own expense and this was immediately accepted by the estate.

Throughout the early part of the 19th century, Fealar continued to be extensively grazed and in 1806 it was reported that a further 135 head of cattle were being sent there, to make the total for that season nearly 500, to be fattened on Fealar grass. The weather appears to have been good at his time as is shown in the factor's report:

We have now had ten days of remarkable fine weather, the country is looking very well and promises an abundant crop. I was at Fealar on Saturday and was astonished at the appearance of the spring there. The vegetation is full and as forward as at Blair, owing to the ground being so compleatly covered till very lately. The day I was there [17 April] it was uncommonly warm.[6]

It must be remembered that Fealar stands at 1,800 feet above sea level, which makes this all the more remarkable.

The lodge was burgled in 1822, when eighteen bottles of claret were drunk or removed and porter, hams and other items were taken away. There was some concern at the time about the number of thieves in the district and they were described as "quite formidable particularly as they seem to be mostly Irish".[7] Instances of poaching were also on the increase and one incident in 1813 tells of six men, four with double-barrelled shotguns, who were seen shooting at deer near the county boundary, two miles from the lodge.

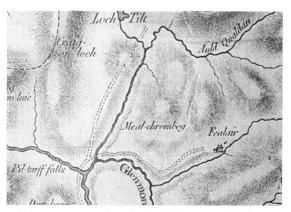

Extract from "Counties of Perth and Clackmannan" by James Stobie, 1783, showing Fealar and the old track from Glen Tilt.

Poaching

Another such incident occurred in October 1822, when two poachers, one armed with a shotgun, were spotted on the march and immediately challenged by James Macfarlane, a Fealar keeper, who asked them to give him their names and addresses. This the poachers declined to do, so the keeper followed at a safe distance until the poachers halted and one "swore if he followed him any further he would shoot him, and actually took aim and discharged one of his barrels at Macfarlane's legs, which did not hurt him very much". Frightened for his life, Macfarlane fell back and eventually lost the men in hill fog.[8] After this it was decided to base James Macfarlane permanently in John Farquharson's bothy at Daldhu, as a deterrent to poachers approaching Fealar from Glenfernate.

On 31 August 1825, Humphrey Christie, one of the Fealar keepers, said he had come upon three men with guns and when he approached them, was shot in the leg. Four days later a full account was given to the factor:

... about 3 o' clock after hearing some firing, he discovered three men at some distance and made up with two of them, the other having layed down or disappeared, but not before he could discover he was wearing a blue bonnet, blue coat and pantaloons and carried a game bag apparently containing more game.

The other two wore same dress ... Each had a double barrel of the largest size and had leather belts, shot bag and powder flask. The one about 5 feet 11 inches high, stout made and dark complexioned. The other about 5 feet 8 inches high also stout made and dark. They had with them a dark brown pointer dog answering to the name "Rover". When within 50 yards of them one of them called out to him "What do you want here?" Christie answered he was here on his duty and demanded of them what right they had to be there. One of the poachers replied, "I shall soon show that" and immediately presented his gun, took aim and discharged one of the barrels, lodging part of the contents in his left leg, above and below the knee. He swore he would give him the contents of the other barrel if he did not immediately make off and then presented the other barrel intending to fire but the pin snapped without flashing the powder. The same person swore if he didn't get up and make off that he would blow his brains out as he lay. He [Christie] for fear of his life rose up and went some distance and saw the third man rejoin them and the whole went off together.[9]

The Duke was very concerned about this assault and injury to one of his keepers and arranged for Dr Stewart from Blair Atholl to examine him, who afterwards reported:

> This is to certify that I have examined Humphrey Christie and extracted a small leaden drop from under the skin a little below the calf of the left leg. There was the appearance as if another had entered the thigh about four inches above the knee joint attended with considerable discolouration of the skin but the wound was so much healed that I could not discern whether there was a leaden drop in it or not and these are all the injuries that were pointed out to me.[10]

The factor went to great lengths to establish the identity of the alleged poachers but could find no one who believed the attack and came to the conclusion the story was a fabrication. The Duke also was convinced that not a word of Christie's report was true, saying that the "circumstances were too unlikely to gain credit".

The arrival of the railway at Perth provided great opportunities for the marketing and dispatching of poachers' gains and it was said in 1851 that "poaching has been carrying on to a fearful extent. So much as 5 and 6 hundredweight of grouse have been forwarded in a day to London by the goods train from Perth." Apparently two boxes containing fifty brace of birds were seized. These had been netted at night, wrapped in cartridge paper and peppered for preservation. The authorities were confident the culprits would be caught and fined £5 for each bird and failure to pay the penalty would result in two months imprisonment for each bird stolen.

Troublesome Tenant

Problems with Horatio Ross, the tenant in 1828, arose not only while he was applying for the lease, but also during his let. As soon as he arrived he complained that whereas his lease said there would be twenty six "cotton counterpanes" in the lodge, there were in fact two only. The factor commented that Ross had misread the inventory and mistaken the "c" of cotton for the "6" in 26. Previous tenants had been quite satisfied and "if we give way to every trifling demand for blankets, crockery, pepper pots etc, which are constantly made, this would amount to a heavy tax in many ways", he concluded.[11]

Another problem arose when Ross asked Mr Robertson of the Tilt Inn in (Old) Bridge of Tilt to send up wood and peats as his supplies were

Three Highland ponies in Fealar forest in 1994 with Danny Forbes.

nearly exhausted. He had not been informed that the gate on the Glen Tilt road had been locked and would not be re-opened until the Duke left the castle in two weeks time. "If the Duke's servants in Forest Lodge would not allow any cart to pass he would immediately leave Filaar and not pay one shilling of rent", Ross wrote. The Duke was quite unperturbed by this threat and replied:

> The public road to Fealar was still open. The carriage drive had been open to Forest Lodge for only two months and had been so misused by the passage of vehicles etc to Felar that the gate on it had been closed. A baggage cart had been allowed through only on the day when permission was sought. Carts with fuel would be allowed through if permission is asked.[12]

Since Ross's letter had been delivered to the castle by a "casual herd", the Duke sent his reply by a shepherd.

Shortage of game reached crisis point in the 1850s, with one tenant complaining that there were no grouse on the Fealar Moors "and like the Bengal Sepoy Army the grouse on these fine hills, that I hear used to swarm with them, have ceased to exist". He stated that after a shoot lasting 4 to 5 hours, his bag was only 5½ brace and blamed the previous season's shooting when too many old birds had been killed. Another reason he gave was disease that had "cleared the ground" and his solution was to prohibit all shooting for the next 2 to 3 years.[13] Donald Robertson, the keeper, concurred, stating that he had shot only 13 brace throughout August and that unless it stopped, grouse would be "extirpated". Matters did improve and in the season of 1867/68, 5 stags, 11 hinds, 1 fallow deer and 1,492 brace of grouse were shot.

Further Repairs

By 1830 Fealar Lodge again required urgent repairs as a report to the factor revealed that the roof was in a very bad state of repair and the three main rooms were flooded. The attached shepherd's house and stables were in a similar condition and if not repaired "they will soon be in ruins". The kennels too, were in a deplorable state and "not fit for pigs".[14]

Urgent repairs were carried out but by 1844 there were further problems of a very serious nature, according to a survey dated 19 May:

> ... we have gone and examined Filar Shooting Lodge and our opinion upon it is that in its present state it is quite unfit to be inhabited by any respectable person. The walls present a very tattered and in many places a very unsound appearance. A great part of the plasterwork inside is come off and much more would require to be taken off and renewed. The deal floors however are all good. Doors and windows are, with few exceptions also good and the principal timbers of the roof are likewise sufficient. The whole roof would require to be slated anew and all the most dangerous parts of the wall taken down and rebuilt. Probable cost £90 Sterling.[15]

Hasty repairs were again undertaken, so that the lodge was ready to be advertised for let for the 1846 season. The following advertisement appeared in several newspapers:

FALLAR

> A first rate quota for grouse and ptarmigan and equal in extent to 4 or 5 guns. If desired by the tenant a right to kill a limited number of red deer would be given on certain conditions. There is a comfortable furnished lodge on the ground.[16]

More extensive advertising appeared in the 1880s when the lodge was leased for three years at an annual rent of £1,900 exclusive of the gamekeepers' wages along with public rates which were about £166. Tenants were responsible for the maintenance of the lodge and were to provide their own furniture. Stags could be shot only between 1 August and 10 October, with hinds betweeen these dates and from 1 November to 1 February, when a maximum of twenty could be culled.

Lodge Rebuilt

It was not until 1911 that plans were made to rebuild and enlarge the lodge extensively. Much of the existing central part remained but two wings were added. One contained a new drawing room, 20 feet by 18 feet, with a bay window. To the rear there was a new entrance with porch, lobby and hallway, while elsewhere on the ground floor there was a coal and peat house and place for ash. Above this there was a new double bedroom with an adjacent dressing room. In the other new wing, a gun room, 21 feet by 11 feet was built with an external door and the dining room was extended. All double beds were to be not less than 5 feet wide, while guests' single beds were 3 feet 3 inches wide and servants' beds 3 feet wide. The enlarged lodge could accommodate three married couples, with two dressing rooms, a single guest and six maids. Additionally the annexe could put up two gentlemen with their servants.[17]

Bothies

At one time there were two bothies, at opposite ends of the Fealar forest. The Lochain Bothy, appearing on maps as **Bothan an Lochain** 982 782 is on the east bank of the Lochain Burn near to where it joins the Tilt. It was built about 130 years ago and was subsequently burned down leaving substantial remains. Close to the county march with Aberdeenshire and south-west of Carn Bhac are the remains of the bothy called **Carn a' Bhutha** (hill of the booth) 035 822, named after the nearby ridge. Here the gable ends are still complete, with a fireplace as a reminder of the severe weather experienced in those remote hills, even in summer. As with many other hill bothies on the march, this one became a watcher's bothy against poaching.

Sale of Fealar

After the First World War, in the 1920s, the Atholl estate was desperately short of cash, so it was agreed that a number of shooting lodges and deer forests should be sold off to reduce the debt burden. The Duke refused to consider parting with either Dalnamein or Kindrochet, but agreed to dispose of Dalnaspidal, Dalnacardoch and Fealar, which was first proposed for sale in 1926.

In 1934, a stockbroker, Mr Alexander Spearman, from Gresham Street, London, was the Fealar tenant and made a tentative offer to purchase for £6,250 based on ten years' rental at £650 per annum. He thought that Fealar was regarded by the estate as an "excrescence or protuberance" and would be glad to be rid of it for about £5,000. The factor disagreed with the offered price, saying that a value equivalent to sixteen or eighteen times the annual rent was more realistic. Negotiations continued along these lines for several months and when Alexander Spearman raised his offer to £10,000, that was on the basis that 2,000 acres on the west side of the Tilt were included in the sale. The estate opposed this on the grounds that this particular land lay "more naturally with the Atholl forest" and that the Tilt was a natural boundary. In March 1935 a settlement agreeable to both sides was reached and the factor noted he was "sorry to see Fealar go but at any rate the west side of Allt Garbh Buidhe has been secured meantime". The disposition which was dated 15 May 1935, stated that for £6,250 the ground was "that part of the Forest of Atholl lying wholly to the east side of Glen Tilt forming the major part of lands formerly known as the deer forest of Fealar extending to 12,500 acres ..."[18]

Fealar Keeper

To come up to date, the gamekeeper and shepherd at Fealar until 1995 was Jimmy Lean,

Jimmy Lean, the former Fealar keeper, sitting by the site of the old Fealar illicit still, half a mile from the lodge.

whose home, at a height of 1,800 feet, must make it one of the highest inhabited houses in Scotland. It lies fourteen miles from the nearest main road, along a rough and twisting track, past towering peaks, some of which are over 3,000 feet and at times with twenty- foot snowdrifts the track can be impassible from November to the end of April. Jimmy spent all his working life in the glen, starting first as a shepherd in Glenfernate, nearly fifty years ago and was the Fealar keeper for twelve years. Fealar is a hind forest, where the hinds come to calve and two hundred are culled every year, along with up to a hundred stags while the grouse bag amounted to around 400 - 500 brace in the season.

The illicit copper still from Fealar is now housed in Blair Castle.

When the Marquis of Waterford was a tenant at Fealar around 1800, he decided to play a trick on a self-invited guest. Seeing a party of tinkers near the lodge he offered to buy their donkey for £5, which was eagerly accepted. The "friend" went off, accompanied by one of the keepers for a deer stalk and after much crawling across a peat bog, he aimed at a pair of horns he had seen earlier through the glasses. The immediate response was a pitiful hee-haw, as the antlers had been attached to the poor donkey's head.[19]

SEVEN SHIELINGS AND LUDE FORESTS

The Seven Shielings forest, formerly known as Freechrombie and sometimes as the Ben Vuirich forest, is situated to the south west of Fealar. It is centred on Loch Loch and was the subject of intense litigation over several centuries between the Robertson lairds of Lude and the Atholl estate. The basic problem which gave rise to this was, that whereas Lude owned the grazing rights, Atholl was the feudal superior of the land in question and this situation remained unresolved for hundreds of years. In a charter of 1669, Lude was granted the rights of fowling, hunting and fishing across the Seven Shielings and was permitted to cultivate them in any way he wished. For these rights he paid two sheep for each of the shielings. The document stated that : "Robertson [of Lude] is to hold the lands freely, immunely, entirely and wholly without any hindrance to be made good".[1]

This arrangement did not apply to a shieling called **Ruidh na Cuile** (windy shieling) 985 758, which lay just outside the area, on a gently rising grassy slope below Meall Reamhar at the north end of Loch Loch. This was a large shieling where the remains of nearly thirty circular and rectangular bothies are still visible. The Marquis of Atholl was determined to establish his rights

to this shieling because its use for pasturing cattle obstructed the passage of deer between his two forests of Fealar and Beinn a' Ghlo. When he lost his claim to it in a court case heard on 6 February 1679, he formed an armed force called the "Watch" under the pretext of keeping the country peaceful and lawful, and the keeping of the forest was committed to their care. On 3 July 1680, the captain of the "Watch" encroached on the shieling and built a small hut on it, which was promptly removed by Lude tenants who "did make civil interruption by casting down of certain divots [turfs] and timbers of the said bothie". In June 1687 the bothy was secretly rebuilt but was promptly demolished by Lude once more.[2]

Litigation

More litigation followed in 1687, when, at the Atholl Court of Regality in Blair Castle, Lude produced a number of witnesses to prove his right to the shieling. One of them, Robert Gray, then 86 years old, knew that it belonged to Lude and said that at one time there were 12 men working there in the summer. Another, John Robertson from Straloch, aged 70, said the

An aerial view of Loch Loch, at the centre of the Seven Shielings area. It is possible to wade across it at the narrow part in the foreground.

shieling had been worked by Lude tenants for over fifty years without interruption, until the previous three years. The dispute continued, being raised again in 1697, when a deposition by eight old gamekeepers was given in Blair Castle, with the same result - Atholl did not own the grazing rights to the shieling - and this situation remained until 1716.

Lude tenants continued to work the Seven Shielings without hindrance until 1715 and the Jacobite rising, in which Lude's brother, Alexander Robertson of Carnoustie took part, was captured and imprisoned in Blair Castle. Any application to free him was useless, as Atholl insisted on a payment of £10,000 Scots (£833.6.8 Sterling) for his freedom. Unable to meet this and desperate to save his brother's life, Lude at length agreed to new rights and conditions being imposed on the Seven Shielings, resulting in his having only a bare servitude of pasture for three months each year. On 5 December 1716 a decreet was signed which contained the following clauses:

1. Although formerly the boundary was along the tops of the mountains, a new line would be drawn about the middle of the face of the hill.
2. Lude's tenants must observe the normal times of going to and leaving their shielings which was 1 May to 1 August.
3. Lude's tenants were prevented from keeping a dog on the shielings.
4. The shielings were for pasture only and nothing else.
5. Tenants were restricted from tilling and labouring.
6. Lude had to pay two wedders (sheep) for each shieling.
7. Whenever Atholl intended to hunt over this land, Lude's tenants had to remove themselves and their animals at least eight days beforehand and were not allowed to return for a further eight days.
8. Atholl had sole rights to fishing on the loch and also for fowling.
9. Atholl gamekeepers were empowered to impound any beasts found pasturing outside the march.[3]

These clauses imposed strict and severe limitations on the use of the shielings. Lude maintained that for many years it had been the practice to take their cattle up to the shielings in the spring as soon as the snow had receded and at the approach of harvest they would bring down their milk cows but leave their yeld cattle (without milk) until November. As far as the absence of dogs was concerned, it was impossible to herd sheep and cattle and prevent them from straying without them. Dogs were essential for the management of livestock.

About the same time, Atholl enlisted the help

An extract from a 1761 document which names each of the Seven Shielings.

of Aeneas Macpherson from Killiehuntly in Glen Tromie, to whom he had granted a very favourable lease of Fealar. Aeneas agreed to act as the middle man and arranged that, in return for his brother's complete freedom, Lude would relinquish all rights to Ruidh na Cuile.

There were no further developments until 1758, when, as the spring weather was favourable, everyone travelled to the shielings early and were dismayed to learn that Atholl gamekeepers were seizing and impounding their livestock. Lude considered this to be "plainly unwarrantable" and the next year both parties agreed to submit the dispute to arbitration. Lude's legal submission was prepared well within the given time, but Atholl was unable to produce enough evidence to support his claim and after many delays, insisted that a sole arbiter be appointed, or the whole matter would be raised in the House of Lords. Lude, dreading the uncertain consequences of another lengthy and expensive lawsuit, reluctantly agreed and John Mackenzie of Delvine (who was appointed Atholl's lawyer in 1762) became the arbiter and a new submission was prepared, giving him sole powers over the outcome.

1761 Decreet

The decreet of 1761 produced results totally different from what Lude had expected, as it contained a number of clauses additional to those in the 1716 case, which were:

If the shieling times were extended a financial penalty would be imposed.

Yearly payment of two sheep per shieling should be converted to a cash sum.

Any animals found in the shieling pasture outside accepted times would be seized and impounded.

Lude tenants had no right to cast peats or dig firr (roots used as candles).

Only bothies or huts could be built in the shielings as the building of better houses would bring more people to the area thus damaging the forest and its game.

> The bothies that is in the practice of being built are commonly no better than to last one season the walls being built only with feal [turf]. Perhaps by reparation they may serve two seasons but that is the most.[4]

Lude observed at the time that "these and other unacceptable clauses must render this sentence far from being a final one and it appears to be rather the groundwork of future discontent and litigation". This unhappy situation was never properly resolved but at the start of the nineteenth century Lude gained sole pasture rights to the Seven Shielings which commenced on 1 May and terminated on 1 September, with yeld cattle remaining until 1

November. However, Atholl still retained the right to hunt across the shielings, but not before 1 September.

First Gamekeeper

At the start of the eighteenth century the first gamekeeper of the Seven Shielings was Thomas Mackenzie, from Rienakyllich above Killiecrankie, and he was followed by Alexander Stewart of Innerslanie in Glen Tilt, who was also in charge of the Tarf forest. He was given the following instructions on 20 November 1712:

> You are to preserve our deer and for that end you are carefully and exactly to observe keep and perform all and every of the instructions relative heirto ... and to assist those of our fforesters when there is occasion. You are to kill yearly twenty deer for our use in our said fforest of Ffriechromby all of which we hereby give you full power warrand and commission and for your encouragement and pains heirin we allow you ffourty merks Scots [£2.4.5 Sterling] of yearly salary beginning the first payment of the same at Martinmas.[5]

Alex was a staunch Jacobite supporter and was taken prisoner after the Battle of Sheriffmuir in 1715, so that his job was given to John MacIntosh from Edenmharkie in Badenoch.

Hunting

In 1801 Atholl planned a massive hunt or tinchel, which was to take place across the shielings, so Lude's tenants were duly ordered to remove their families and livestock. Announcements were made at St Bride's church in Old Blair and several hundred men reported in their finery, as commanded, on the morning of the intended hunt. Many of the Duke's friends and neighbouring lairds had been invited and asked to bring as many hounds as possible, since the Atholl kennels could not meet the requirement. Such a spectacle had not been seen for many years as hundreds of men forgathered on the Seven Shielings, "but none of them had the least conception of what was to be their employment. They had heard from their fathers and grandfathers that ... the country had been raised, and the deer encircled and killed" and a contemporary report described the outcome:

> ... A great number of ropes had been provided, which this convocation were ordered to carry along with them. Their instructions were to proceed to the natural resort of the deer in his Grace's forest grounds, and, when there, to separate as far from each other as they could keep the ropes they carried with them stretched or suspended at a proper height. In this way, a line, extending for several miles, and including a very large tract of ground, was formed; and orders to form into a semi-circle being issued, this immense machine moved on towards Lude's grazings, with the view of forcing every deer that happened to be in the course of its progress, to appear on the pasture grounds of Lude, for the purpose of being hunted

Stags in the Seven Shielings. (Roger Lee)

there. In the meantime, his Grace, attended by a numerous host, having for a rear-guard the hounds collected from various kennels, proceeded to the pasture grounds of Lude, hoping that the devoted victims, for the day, would there appear; but while neither means nor expence were spared to make the spectacle worthy of those who came far and near to behold it, the beasts of the field spurned at the unnatural restraint attempted to be imposed on them. Not a single deer could be brought to the pasture grounds of Lude; and those who had assembled to witness *a grand deer hunting* were disappointed ...[6]

The Duke was not deterred by this total failure and Atholl continued to hunt across the Seven Shielings for the next fifty years, albeit on a less ambitious scale.

Poaching

Poaching was as rife in the Lude forests as in any of the others and sometimes it was even the gentry themselves who were caught out. John Menzies from Menzies Hill was most concerned in 1761, to hear that the Duke was considering a prosecution against him for shooting in the Atholl forest. His excuse was that after a day's shooting on Invercauld land, he and his friends finished up a few miles from Fealar, where Lord Kinnaird asked them to stay the night in the lodge. The next day they were invited to join

him on a shoot in Glen Loch, as he assured them he had approval to do this. "It's the first time I ever fell into a scrape of this kind, for I make it a point never to hunt on any ground without liberty", he concluded and the Duke relented.[7]

In 1802 Atholl keepers caught six poachers on the Seven Shielings but it was discovered that Lude had given them permission and employed a Perth lawyer, Mr Stewart, to defend them. The Atholl factor was appalled and wrote furiously:

> I could not have thought it possible that any person possessing the character of a gentleman could have been concerned in such shameful business, by putting himself at the head of and attempting to defend a set of poachers guilty of trespassing against the laws of their country and encouraged by him to do so. However I hope they will soon meet the punishment they deserve and if possible Lude must be made a party, at any event his conduct has undergone a public investigation, and I dont think he will obtain much applause by his interference.[8]

The defendants were found guilty under several acts of parliament, namely that "they did pursue a herd of deer each having a gun and did shoot and kill or wound a deer and likewise shoot a muirfowl". Also, "they did this without having a certificate required by the Act of Parliament". A. Fraser, A. Robertson, R. Robertson, R. McLauchlin and A. Stewart were found guilty and each fined £10. Jim Robertson, a persistent offender, was fined £20 and all were given the option of spending three months in Perth prison for non payment of their fines.[9]

Humphrey Sturt

In August 1811 the Duke took out a summons against a Lude shooting tenant, Humphrey Sturt, who persisted in shooting across the Seven Shielings, again with the alleged knowledge and encouragement of General Robertson, the laird of Lude. The Atholl factor instigated an investigation into Sturt's activities and found he was guilty on two counts. In the first instance he had been seen shooting a partridge on the Haugh of Blair and killing hares in Tulach Park, opposite the castle. Secondly, he had sent out his gamekeeper and servant to shoot a deer which was carried on a cart to Sturt's house on Lude. Apparently it had been dragged across Atholl ground on to Toldunie and then taken away. When John Paul Robertson, the Lude gamekeeper was interviewed, he confessed it was he who had shot the deer, but only under duress from Sturt, who had sent along his servant to ensure his orders were carried out. As the Atholl keepers returned from their investigations they drove all the deer away from Lude's land, "to prevent them being killed by the Ludites".[10]

Humphrey Sturt's counsel drew up answers to the Duke's allegations and maintained that he had not trespassed nor shot on Atholl land but shot grouse on "the pasture grounds of Lude, where that family and their keepers have killed grouse time out of mind." He insisted that this privilege was included in the lease granted to him by General Robertson and went on to say that:

> The Duke's only right there [Seven Shielings] is that of hunting deer, which is not the same as grouse shooting and this is a personal privilege to the Duke himself and does not permitt his factor and others to shoot grouse there or to pasture horses.

These were strong words, highlighting the difficulties of prosecuting alleged poachers, especially when they were defended by an astute lawyer. In this case the defence was concluded with an assertive proposition: "Under the circumstances the respondent considers the presenting of the Petition a rash measure and we can entertain no doubt that your Lordship will recall the Interdict and subject the Petitioner with full costs."[11]

The Duke backed off from this confrontation and the case was withdrawn.

There was consternation in Atholl in August 1817 when two men, Mr Arnot, a lawyer and Mr Stainton, an advocate, were spotted on the Seven Shielings, as four years earlier they had shot every bird in sight, causing great havoc. The Atholl lawyer, John Rutherford was authorised to dispatch an interdict to the sheriff to prevent them from shooting over the Atholl deer forests and a constable was commissioned to deliver this as soon as possible.

Towards the end of the nineteenth century two well-known poachers stalked a magnificent stag on the hill face above Creag an Loch, on the east side of Loch Loch and were successful in bringing it down. Their trophy turned out to be a Royal (12 points) and after gralloching it they concealed the carcase, as they were unsure whether they had been observed or not. Two nights later one of them returned with a deer pony and waited below the spot where the stag had been hidden, while the other made straight for it. As they had feared, there were three or four keepers concealed in the heather waiting for them, who chased after the poacher but found it impossible to catch such an athlete, who earlier in the year had won the hill race at the Glen Isla games. Having made sure that all the keepers were in full pursuit of his colleague, the other poacher calmly led his pony up the hill, tied the stag on to its back and set off at a quick pace to safety.[12]

Shielings

Cattle were very important to the Highland economy and their milk, buttermilk, butter and cheese formed not only a major part of the staple diet of the inhabitants but constituted a large part of their rent. Glen Loch enjoyed rich pasture and at the end of the eighteenth century nearly sixty families tended their livestock and lived in the shieling bothies in the summer months. It must have been a busy, active place in those days, with the glen echoing to the voices and laughter of the children. By the early nineteenth century the emphasis had turned to sheep and in some seasons as many as 3,500 sheep grazed in the glen. Now the glen is left to the sheep and deer and the whole area is empty of human life.

Ruidh Sron nan Dias (shieling of the point of the blade) 994 729 is the most northerly of the Seven Shielings and is situated at the south end of Loch Loch 1,500 feet up on the ridge which gives it its

The wooden bothy at Ruidh Chuilein, used as a ponyman's bothy until it burned down in 1993.

name. John Robertson from Middlebridge in Glenfender worked here as a herd boy in the 1780s and recorded that the snow often lay for many months and sometimes well into May when the shieling season had already started. A bothy which was built here in the nineteenth century as a place of refuge in times of storm, is marked on modern maps.

Ruidh-chuilein (shieling of the whelp) 994 717 is situated on the glen floor, where the footings of at least eight shieling bothies can still be seen but there were many more at one time, because at least fourteen families are recorded as living here in the eighteenth century. There used to be a wooden hut situated here, which was used as a lunch hut for shooting parties and also as a shelter for the ponyman but it was burnt down by vandals in the spring of 1993.

Aldnaherry (stream of broken ground) 957 687 was paradoxically described as the best pasture in the area "because of the nature of the soil". It was situated below Allt Loch Valigan, where visible remains of fifteen shieling bothies are to be found.

Creagan Gorm (little green rocky place), 976 677, located on a rocky knoll which dominates the surrounding area, is another of the Seven Shielings. Several bothy remains are still visible here and in 1680 the tenant paid two salmon, worth twenty shillings Scots as the rent for pasturing his cattle here. Creagan Gorm is at the south end of the Seven Shielings and Atholl went to extreme measures to ensure that Lude tenants were well aware of the boundary of their grazing area. As this area is largely featureless, he erected eight march stones, each marked AL for both lairds and clearly numbered. The locations

Stone AL 2 on the Atholl/Lude boundary, beside Allt na Leacainn Moire.

The fourth stone on the Atholl/Lude grazing march.

of these stones are shown on James Stobie's map "Plan of Blair ..."[13] dated 1780, while a 1763 document describes the boundary in detail:

> From a stone or large boulder on Craiglachanach marked AL 1 in a straight line running south-west to a point in the Water of Brerachan where a stone marked AL 2 has been set up at my sight on the left bank of said water from thence up the said Water of Brerachan to the north side of Stronadruim to a large stone at the waterside marked AL 3 from thence in a straight line one hundred and fifty-seven yards west north west to a stone at the foot of Druiminagach marked AL 4 from there in a straight line seven hundred and seven yards north by east past a stone marked AL 5 to a stone in a hollow at the foot of Knockvalon marked AL 6 from thence in a straight line five hundred and seventy yards north-east to a rock marked on top thereof AL 7 from thence in a straight line five hundred and fifty yards north by east to a rock marked AL 8 and from thence in a straight line to the top of Knockbreakmore.[14]

Four Atholl keepers in 1856:
Left to Right: Robert Stewart; unknown; Donald McGlashan; Robert McNaughton.

At least seven of these rocks remain, standing mute sentinel to the centuries-long struggle over grazing rights between Lude and Atholl.

GLENFERNATE

Glenfernate adjoins the Seven Shielings to the east and the lower half was purchased by the Atholl estate in 1825. Then it consisted of 3,364 acres of hill pasture and 684 acres of arable ground. The sale particulars described it as being:

> ... for the best part well enclosed, levelled, subdivided and in a good state of cultivation; and the Grazings are allowed to be superior for all kinds of stock to any others of the same extent in Perthshire, or even in the Highlands of Scotland.

> There is a small, but neat Mansion House, in good repair, and agreeably situated; also a suitable set of offices and garden. The grounds in their vicinity are embellished with belts of fir planting; and there are a few acres of natural wood along the banks of the Water of Fernate. The property abounds with game of every description ...

> From these premises the sale of this fine property has been estimated by proper judges at about £22,500. To leave room for competition however, it is to be offered so low as £20,000.[15]

Negotiations to purchase started in July of that year, when George Condie, Atholl's Perth lawyer, was instructed to offer £17,000 and was told that an additional £1,000 would secure the sale. Soon afterwards the purchase for £18,000, from Captain Grant of Kilgraston went through, with the added sum of £1,164 for the furniture in the lodge and some livestock, mainly sheep.[16]

Gordon McGregor, a keeper for 25 years, and for the past 8 of them, head keeper for the Glenfernate and Seven Shielings forests.

Glenfernate, combined with the Seven Shielings, formed an extensive shooting area, which in the 1880s was under the control of John Macbeath as head keeper. The game bag for the 1884/85 season comprised as follows: hind 2; roe 1; grouse 1,339; ptarmigan 24; woodcock 7; snipe 7; plover 3; white hare 46; rabbit 10; fox 22; weasel 27; hoodie crow 9 and hawk 2.[17]

On Lude estate, looking towards Shinagag from the old sheep roundel near Tomnabroilach.

Glenfernate, with part of the Seven Shielings, was sold off on 12 July 1927 to Mr John Heathcote Amory, whose family had leased the estate since the end of the nineteenth century. The price of £32,250 included the lodge, forest and shieling of Ruidh nan Laogh.

LUDE FOREST

For centuries, the estate of Lude, which comprised some 12,000 acres had belonged to a cadet (junior) branch of the Robertsons of Struan, the chiefs of Clan Donnachaidh. By the nineteenth century its shooting was primarily for grouse and when it came up for sale in 1820 its "Particulars of Sale" described it as follows:

> Throughout the whole extent, the estate rests on a bed of primitive limestone and marble, rendering the pasture superior in quality to most in the Highlands, while the arable land, being of a rich loam, is capable of returning the weightiest and best grain of all sorts, as well as green crops. The crops of hay both from natural and sown grasses, are nowhere to be surpassed.

> The low grounds are, for the most part, inclosed and subdivided by substantial stone fences, completely drained and levelled and sheltered and embellished with thriving plantations. The marble is of the same description as that in Glen Tilt, with easier access and shorter carriage; and the lime is of the best quality, and in demand in the neighbourhood for a considerable distance ...

> The estate abounds with grouse and game of every description and is constantly frequented by red and roe deer from the adjoining forest of Atholl ...[18]

A list of game killed on Lude between July 1859 and February 1860 is as follows: grouse 53½ brace; snipe 16; wild duck 11; partridge 24½ brace; plover 10; woodcock 1; pheasant 12; red deer 3; roe deer 2; hare 113; rabbit 1,298.[19]

Lude estate was purchased by its present owner, Major W G Gordon in 1938 and since then a number of additions, including part of the

Seven Shielings and Loch Valigan have been made. In the nineteenth century Loch Valigan was a small beat on the Atholl estate under the charge of a gamekeeper called Thomas Mitchie and in the 1884/85 season a total of 456 brace of grouse were shot there. Grouse shooting peaked across the whole of the Lude estate in 1901 when the season's bag totalled 1,065 brace. Along with

Alister Stephen has been the keeper on Lude estate for the past 14 years.

most other estates in the area, the grouse population has declined dramatically, but this has been more than offset by great improvements in deer stalking, with Lude now being a deer forest in its own right as up to a hundred stags are shot in the season.

Bothies

Creag-Choinneach Lodge (mossy crag) 919 703 stands on a rocky outcrop on the south west slope of Carn Liath high up on the east side of the Fender Burn. It was built by Mr McInroy of Lude in the 1820s for use in times of grouse shooting. It was also used as a base from which stalking from Atholl might be disturbed, since Atholl had placed deer watchers in **Lyncondlich** 924 658 in Glen Girnaig and **Daldhu** 025 705 in Glen Fernate to deter deer from entering Lude ground and this was seen as a reciprocal counter measure. **Shinagag** (old pass) 953 673 lies at the end of a rough track, eight miles distant from Blair Atholl and was a notable hill farm at one time. Now it is occasionally used by shepherds in summer, when up to 800 ewes are clipped.

Loch Valigan, nearly 2,000 feet above sea level, and a favoured spot for nesting gulls, with Carn nan Gabhar, the highest of the Beinn a' Ghlo peaks, at nearly 3,700 feet, in the background.

TARF FOREST

The Tarf forest was due west of Fealar and ten miles in length. Now it is part of the Tilt forest, although one hundred and seventy years ago it was let out to Sir David Moncreiffe for £100, as a separate hunting beat. It straddled the Tarf Water, with the Aberdeenshire county boundary to the north and Loch Tilt and Allt Garbh Buidhe forming the eastern march. To the west it terminated in a deer sanctuary. Every well-managed forest included at least one deer sanctuary and Atholl was no exception. No shot was ever fired in it and the deer seemed to know they were safe, with even wounded beasts making for it as if to seek protection. It is difficult to pin-point the reason for its location, except that it was veryisolated and even nowadays is a three and a half hour walk from the nearest dropping-off point.

In 1667 the Earl of Atholl complained to his cousin, the Earl of Fife, in Mar, that his keepers were crossing the forest boundary and shooting game in the Tarf. When challenged, they said they had authority from their master, although the Earl denied it. "The number is verie small", he wrote but agreed that it had to stop.[1] Adjoining landowners often co-operated to reduce poaching and illegal grazing as is shown in Fife's letter to Atholl, dated 21 November 1704 on learning that the Duke had given orders to prevent lowland cattle from grazing in his forests. Fife indicated that he too would issue similar orders and would agree to any other restrictions the Duke decided to impose.[2]

This co-operation between the great neighbouring landowners of Atholl and Mar continued, and along with the Duke of Gordon in Badenoch, they issued a joint proclamation in 1779, which was fixed to church doors to draw attention to the old forest laws and their penalties. Although they admitted amongst themselves that many of these laws were now obsolete, they wished to publicise them, "just to terrify a little".

> ... they will prosecute every unqualified person, hunting on their Properties, and particularly every Person who shall be found hunting in their Forests, killing or destroying the Deer and Roe. They have directed the Foresters to detect all Poachers of Game, and to inform upon all who carry Arms, or bring Dogs within the Bounds of the Forests. They have promised a Reward of TWENTY GUINEAS to any Person who will inform on the Transgressors, the same to be paid upon Conviction of the Offenders.

> It is declared that no man shoot a deer, wild beast, or wild fowl, with gun, or other weapon, under pain of death, and Escheat of Moveables, and the apprehender of the offenders, who brings the offending to the Sheriff, to have the Moveables for a Reward.[3]

This was an enormous sum of money for those

The Tarf Water, 10 miles in length, flows east to join the Tilt at the famous falls.

days; more than most people were paid in a year. One of the laws quoted had been passed in the time of Mary Queen of Scots, when the death penalty was applied to anyone caught shooting "deer, wild beast or wild fowl with gun or other weapon".

Despite these threats and other preventive measures, poaching continued in its various guises, sometimes unexpected. Roualeyn Gordon-Cumming, who later became a famous big-game hunter, spent 29 March 1843 as a guest at Blair Castle. The following day, he, accompanied by three men and four deer-hounds were spied shooting deer in the Tarf forest on their way home. The party had abused Lord Glenlyon's (later the 6th Duke) hospitality by poaching a stag and when challenged, refused to give their names. As he was suspicious, the Fealar keeper checked the Feith Uaine Bothy nearby, where he found a freshly-killed stag. In his report he added that the door of the bothy had been forced, the beds slept in, and strange to record, the intruders had left behind a bottle of whisky!

Gordon-Cumming was uneasy about the outcome of this poaching incident, and fearing the wrath of Lord Glenlyon, wrote a letter of explanation to him when he returned to England:

> I went to your forest in search of eagles' eggs for a collection and killed one stag in Glen Tarf to give a young greyhound blood. I did not suppose that that would be of any great consequence, as you have far too many deer on your ground, at least double, and I knew that you were not at that season hunting that part of the forest. I did not

break into nor occupy your lodge. I occupied a dilapidated building beside the Tarf without door or window and full of snow.[4]

Lord Glenlyon sought legal advice about his chances of a successful prosecution and an Edinburgh lawyer summed up the various acts which were still in force and decided that many of them were unenforceable. This seems to have discouraged him as there are no records of any prosecution.

Early Gamekeepers

There are few records of the early gamekeepers but Thomas Stewart was appointed to be "fforester of the Forest of Tarff betwixt Bruar and Tilt" in 1715 and had to kill 25 deer yearly for the Duke's use.[5] For this he was given the nearby shieling of Leth-chois for pasturing his livestock. In 1739, James Stewart, a son of Stewart of Innerslanie, was given the post and was paid half a crown for each deer killed.

Robert Graham of Fintry was appointed head gamekeeper of the Atholl Forest in 1739 and in 1745 bought the feu of Fealar, with all rights to shooting and fishing, for £200 and a deer or cow, the choice being his, each year. In July 1748 he perambulated the forest of Tarf and wrote a descriptive report of what he saw:

> I travelled through all the Forrest of Tarff and brought in all the deer we found on the skirts of the fforest. There is a better flock of hinds and young deer in the forest than ever tho' nothing like what ought to be or what I wished.

Red Grouse above the Tarf Water. (Roger Lee)

We killed two harts today but they are not at all fat yet. I sent the largest hart for the Duke and the other I brought home with me here. I ordered the fforester to send a deer or two to his Grace last week. Altho they be not fit they make good supe and collops [slices of meat] but the weather here has been so bad that I have not heard if the foresters could be in the hill or if they sent in any deer but after next week I hope the veneson will then be good. I shall endeavour to furnish his Grace with two good deer every week which the season lets and more if his Grace desires it. I find all the country round here had got a rediculous notion that his Grace inclines to give them great liberty for pasturage and travelling and looking after their beasts and I am persuaded that is both very fals and improper. I recommend it to you and the other factors to notify his Grace forresters to be keept as they ought ...[6]

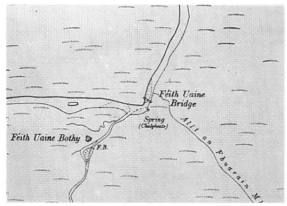

Extract from the 1900 edition of the Ordnance Survey, showing the Feith Uaine Bothy in Glen Tarf.

Feith Uaine Bothy

The Feith Uaine Bothy (green streamlet) 927 789, better known as the Tarf Bothy, is situated about five miles upstream from the Falls of Tarf, above the 1,800 feet contour, at the point where Feith Uaine Mhor joins the Tarf Water. Originally it was a simple building and the earliest reference to its existence is in 1794 when John Forbes from Auchgobhal in Glen Tilt charged 6 shillings for the use of a man and two horses to take baggage to it. When Thomas Palliser, the factor, was visiting the area in 1799, checking cattle in the glen, he reported that the bothy "wanted some repair, a part of the side having fallen in and left the roof in a tottering situation ..."

The factor was told on 4 June 1806 that work to rebuild the bothy completely would start the following Monday "now that sufficient supplies of lime are available". Two months later it was reported that the mason work was finished except for laying the joists and carpenters were about to start on the roof. The following accounts detail the work carried out:[7]

August 1806			
Paid Wm. McEwan for Slates for Tarff Lodge	£ 7	4	0
November 1806			
Paid Wm. Robertson for mason work at Tarff and Bruar Lodges	£36	9	7½
Paid Thos. Stewart plasterer for work at Tarff Lodge	£ 1	12	2
Paid Alex Stewart for two men clearing rubbish from Tarff Lodge	£ 1	0	0
Paid cash for Tenants going with wood to Tarff Lodge	£ 1	11	10
Paid cash for mason labour	£ 3	13	6
April 1807			
Paid Don Clark for Slating Feuwannie Lodge	£ 3	14	6

When the renovations were completed, the lodge consisted of two rooms divided by a chimney-breast and it was occasionally occupied by a deer watcher. However, within twenty years it became a haunt and refuge for poachers and was therefore burnt to the ground by the Atholl hillmen, one of whom was Jock McAra. It remained a ruin until the 1850s when it was rebuilt and re-roofed, this time with thatch and ten years later, was repaired yet again, by Ashley Dodd, the tenant at the time of Forest Lodge. In 1872 it was "by no means a comfortable residence" as there were no floors, ceilings or wall linings and the roof leaked badly. The 7th Duke, longing for some peace and quiet, away from the bustle of Forest Lodge, took it over and had it extensively repaired:

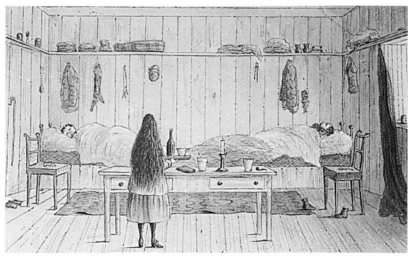

An ink sketch by the 7th Duke in 1875 of one of the Feith Uaine Bothy bedrooms, shows the wood panelling.

1873:   The Lodge was floored, walls wood-lined, a stable built on the east gable and peat house erected on the west side.

1881:   The hillmen's room was constructed into an apartment for the Duchess and the stable fitted up for hillmen accommodation. A new three-stall stable and dog kennel were built and the peat house repaired.[8]

In December 1909 the factor reported a fire in the lodge that caused great damage. Tramps were suspected but there was no proof. Fortunately the building and its contents were fully covered by insurance but Feith Uaine Lodge was once again a ruin and remained so until 1992 when it was repaired by the Scottish Mountaineering Bothy Association. It is now a welcome refuge for climbers and walkers in this remote glen.

Being at the confluence of two rivers, two bridges were needed for access, so two wooden ones were built in 1873. Six years later the Tarf bridge was carried away by ice. It was found a mile downstream, little the worse for wear and was put back. Two years later both bridges were swept away, again by a build-up of ice and as neither were damaged, they were re-installed but this time the Tarf bridge was built in such a way that it could be removed in winter. Despite this, it continued to be swept away and so an aerial ropeway about about forty yards in length was built at a much higher elevation, out of reach of flood levels.[9]

Bedford Bridge

The best-known bridge in the area is the one across the Tarf, below the falls, where it enters the Tilt. The **Bedford Bridge** 983 796 was built in 1886 to commemorate Francis John Bedford, who was drowned whilst attempting to ford the river in 1879. There was however, a single-arch stone bridge built here for the estate in 1776 by John

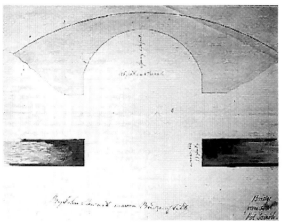

A 1770 plan of the first bridge across the Tarf, near its junction with the Tilt.

Stewart, at a cost of £29.4.0 but this was taken down in 1819 to deter traffic through the glen from Atholl and Deeside.

In 1802 directions were issued for the building of a small bothy a mile to the east of the Tarf Bothy beside Allt a' Chaorainn and below An Sgarsoch, "a situation John Crerar thinks best calculated for a person having charge of the Forest north of Tarf".[10]

This was known as the **Rowan Tree Bothy** 932 797 which was erected under instructions from Lord Waterford, when he was tenant of Fealar and it remained in use until about 1880.

Lord Fife, writing to the Duke in 1896, expressed his views on the duration of the shooting season, maintaining that no stags should be shot after 10 October:

The end of the stag season should be a moveable feast (or rather a fast) as stags vary so much according to the weather. There is not more than one year out of five in which good stags are fit to kill after the 1st week in October. I am absolutely certain that the custom of killing stags late in the season is fatal because good stags at that time can be easely "got" and therefore the race is deteriorating in our forests.[11]

It is impossible to write about this part of Atholl without mentioning the notorious witch of Beinn a' Ghlo as the last reported sighting of her was at a shieling in Glen Tarf. Two poachers from Mar were following a wounded hind when they were overtaken by a savage snowstorm and lost their way. Their meeting with the witch is recorded in McConnachie's *Deer & Deer Forests of Scotland* and in this account she is shown in a rather better light than usual!

...The storm had increased and they were in danger of their lives; they could proceed only with great difficulty, often floundering in the deep soft snow. When their provisions and strength were both quite exhausted they came, to their pleasant surprise, on a shieling. The door opened without their knocking; the forbidding appearance of the woman was passed over when they found a meal had been prepared for them, unexpected guests as they imagined themselves.

By and by their hostess announced herself as the famed witch of Beinn a' Ghlo, she who had power over wind and storm. Producing a rope with three knots in it, she told how the undoing of one sent such a wind as the deerstalker prayed for; another produced a gale; a third, neither man nor beast could withstand the storm. These men, however, were under her protection, and so would remain as they regularly provided her with venison - "If you mean to thrive, ye maun place a fat hart, or a yeld hind, by Fraser's Cairn at midnight, the first Monday in every month, while the season lasts." Worn out with their exertions, the poachers slept soundly on their heather couch; when they awoke no woman was to be seen and the storm had ceased.

A hunting party of 1872 preparing for a day in the hills. They are in front of the recently altered Blair Castle but before the new ballroom had been added. (William Evans)

A herd of deer crossing the Tilt below Forest Lodge in 1856. (William Evans)

"The Fording of the Poll Tarff" in 1861 shows Queen Victoria, Prince Albert and their retinue, the 6th Duke of Atholl and a number of Atholl keepers . (Carl Haag). The Royal Collection © Her Majesty The Queen.
The review of this painting in the "Art Journal" of 1865 stated that "... the figures are most carefully painted ..." The six portraits that follow are copies from original studies made by Carl Haag and the characters are clearly recognisable in the main painting. The copies were given to the Dowager Duchess of Atholl by Queen Victoria when she was staying with her in Dunkeld in 1865.

Two pipers of the Atholl Highlanders; Aeneas Rose, Master of the Dunkeld otter hounds, who was born in 1810 and died in 1880 and Jock Macpherson, gamekeeper, born in 1832 and died in 1905. They are leading the party, immediately behind the guide, Charles Stewart.

Sandy McAra, head gamekeeper from 1847 to 1864, the year that Donald Macbeath took over. Sandy McAra's head is visible behind the Queen.

Donald Macbeath, "the father of the regiment" of the Atholl Highlanders, and a head gamekeeper, who fought with great distinction in the Crimean War. He is to the rear of Prince Albert, leading Princess Alice's horse.

Jock McAra, Sandy McAra's elder brother and also a keeper. He is leading Lady Churchill's horse.

Two Atholl gamekeepers, Jock Robertson, born in 1806 and died in 1879 and Jock Stewart, born in 1825 and died in 1896. Both are easily recognisable on the far left of the painting.

Robert McNaughton, born 1818 and died 1880, leading "Craig Dubh", one of the Duke's ponies, brings up the rear of the cavalcade.

The Feith Uaine Bothy (Tarf), five miles up the glen, was a favourite haunt of the 7th Duke.

Remains of the Rowan Tree Bothy beside Allt a' Chaorainn(Tarf), with the mountain of An Scarsoch in the background.

TILT AND BEINN A' GHLO FOREST

The Tilt forest is the largest in Atholl, covering most of the ground west of the River Tilt, from Gleann Mhairc to the Tarf. It also included most of the Beinn a' Ghlo mountain range to the east.

The whole area abounded in red deer as is borne out in early nineteenth century letters and reports:

18 June 1801 Thomas Palliser, factor
Glen Tilt is looking very well, plenty of fine grass and the ewes and lambs are at the head of the glen ... The deer are very far forward in condition and the high hills are uncommonly green ... I never saw the forest in better order in every respect. There will be a great number of fawns.[1]

6 February 1803 Thomas Palliser, factor
On Friday I went to Forest Lodge ... The whole of the braes are covered with deer, indeed I scarcely could have believed there was so many deer in the forest. Maclaren says he never saw so many deer in Glen Tilt at this season, which he imputes to the glen being so quiet from the tenants being removed from the east side of the Tilt.[2]

In this report, the factor was referring to the leases of the farms of Balaneasie, Alltandubh and Dail na Gaollsaich, which had been terminated the previous year and cleared to make way for sheep.

15 January 1813 Thomas Palliser, factor
There has been a very considerable fall of snow about 18" deep which has stopped all the planting and farming operations. Glen Tilt stock so far has stood the winter very well and are in very good condition as also the red deer but the fallow deer are falling off very fast, in particular last year's fawns ...[3]

27 May 1817 John Crear, head gamekeeper
... I was a night at Forest Lodge. The harts are looking about three weeks better than they had last year at this day. They are getting their new coats on and plenty of them. Those at the green nolls are the farthest forward. The moor game is very plenty and the grass in the glen is looking well.[4]

27 July 1826 Charles Crearar, gamekeeper
The deer is in fine condition this season and plenty of them. Robert Stewart in Auchgobhal tells me there is some fine harts coming into his corn in the night time, and in no hurry in the morning going away. Likewise I saw a number of fine harts in Glen Tilt last week.[5]

These records show up the grazing properties of Glen Tilt, where the abundance of limestone produces good pasture for both deer and domestic livestock.

Glen Tilt from a march stone on the Tilt/Fender commonty boundary.

The first appointment of a gamekeeper in the Atholl forest was recorded on 12 April 1606, when Alexander McIntosh of Tirinie in Glenfender was commissioned by James, Earl of Atholl, to be:

> ... our Forster of the forrest of Beine Cromby [Fealar] and forest of Glentilt, for attending to oure Deir, and that na noylt [cattle], horse nor lowland oxen pasture within the said Forrestis. With Libertie to our Forster to take and apprehend whatsumever horse or oxen sal be fund pasturand therein ...[6]

Alex Stewart of Innerslanie was appointed gamekeeper of the Tilt forest at the end of the seventeenth century. **Innerslanie** 878 696 was a large settlement on the west bank of the Tilt, where the remains of fourteen buildings, two corn-drying kilns and several enclosures are still visible. It became depopulated in 1789 when the ground was turned over to cattle grazing. In 1707 Alex Stewart received orders to "dispossess all persons whatsomever of what sheals they presently possess within our Forests of Atholl". He was also empowered to seize horses, mares and cattle found grazing in the forest and shoot any dogs found, fining the owner of each, twenty shillings Scots.

In August of that same year he was commissioned to captain the guard at the Kilmaveonaig market, with instructions that he was to take a number of armed Fencible men to guard the market at Kilmaveonaig and ensure that law and order were maintained. He was empowered to arrest anyone guilty of "Drunkenness and Swearing until they pay their fynes according to the Laws".[7]

In 1711, as in every year at this time, the Duke held a deer hunt, so Alex Stewart was issued with the following warrant:

> These are empowering Alexander Stewart of Innerslany to take 24 armed men out of Glen Tilt and Dalginross with him tomorrow to the forrest who are hereby ordered to continue with him, obeying his directions, till our deer hunting be over ...[8]

Because of his involvement in the Jacobite uprising of 1715, the 1st Duke was determined to remove Alex Stewart from his land in Glen Tilt, but his younger brother, Lord James Murray of Garth, pleaded for leniency. While Lord James could not say much to mitigate "his crime" (of being a Jacobite) he knew he was very sorry for what he had done. Also, he had a wife and several children who were in great misery with nowhere else to go. Under this pressure the Duke relented but a few years later the factor threatened to take out a summons against Alex Stewart for non payment of his feu duty.

Gable end of Alltandubh 915 723 which was a 25-acre farm in Glen Tilt in 1780.

The Tilt in spate near Clachglas. It is the only river in the area not controlled for hydro electricity. (Ron MacGregor)

Thomas Pennant

In 1769, Thomas Pennant, a gentleman from Flintshire, travelling at a leisurely pace on horseback, visited Scotland for the first time. Having inherited great wealth, he indulged in his passion for travel and noted details of his experiences with great precision. In the fashion of the time these were published in 1774 under the title *A Tour of Scotland 1769*. He was recommended to the Duke by the Earl of Kinnoull at Dupplin, as a personal friend of his brother and very interested in natural history, particularly "animals and minerals". The Earl ended his letter by requesting a guide "to show him the way over the hills to Invercall".[9]

Captain James Murray, brother of the 3rd Duke, acted as his guide and wrote down his experiences on the journey through Glen Tilt:

We arrived here [Invercauld] at a quarter past four ... to satisfy your curiosity in some measure, I think the roade is practicable, tho' not without very great difficulties attending it ... The Roade that is made on your side I take to be about eight measured miles, from thence [to] where you march with Lord Fife upwards of seven. From that thro' Lord Fife's, and he is superior, about twelve miles, and three miles of Invercauld's, which is made and is pretty good. There is about six miles of Lord Fife's made, but it is very bad; it communicates his

upper saw mills with the lower part of Braymar. So by my reckoning there is about 13 miles entirely in the state of nature ... We were about nine hours and a half on horseback; we dined on the side of Loch Tilt. Soon after we got there it began to rain, so we had upwards of four hours of it as heavy as it could pour ... Mr Pennant is very happy to have seen such a roade, but would not wish to undertake it again ...[10]

In his book, Pennant covers in detail his journey up Glen Tilt:

Set out for the county of Aberdeen; ride Eastwards over a hill into Glen-Tilt, famous in old times for producing the most hardy warriors; is a narrow glen, several miles in length, bounded on each side by mountains of an amazing height ...

He then records how they climbed a steep hill and refreshed themselves with goats' whey at a shieling:

Ascend a steep hill and find ourselves on an Arrie, or tract of mountain which the families of one or two hamlets retire to with their flocks for pasture in summer. Here we refreshed ourselves with some goats' whey, at a sheelin, or Bothay, a cottage made of turf, the dairy-house, where the Highland shepherds, or graziers, live with their herds and flocks, and during the fine season make butter and cheese. Their whole furniture consists of a few horn-spoons, their milking utensils, a couch formed of sods to lie on, and a rug to cover them. Their food oat-cakes, butter or cheese, and often the coagulated blood of their cattle spread on their bannocks. Their drink whey, and sometimes by way of indulgence, whisky ...

To avoid the ford at the Falls of Tarf, Pennant was taken along a track called the Dunmore Walk. They passed on the way the shieling of **Ruidh Feith an Duin** (shieling of the streamlet of the hill) 971 785, named after the nearby hill of Dun Mor, where substantial remains of at least seven buildings are still to be found.

When he returned home in September, Pennant wrote to the Duke to acknowledge his gratitude for the kindness shown to him during his visit to Atholl and again, on 20 December 1771 he sent the Duke a copy of his book with the accompanying letter:

> Give me leave to present your Grace with a copy of my tour thro Scotland as a poor mark of the memory I have of the hospitable reception I met at Atholl House [Blair Castle] and the favours I received since. I flatter myself that your Grace will think my engraver has done justice to the drawings ...[11]

The drawings mentioned in the letter were executed by Moses Griffith, who accompanied Pennant on most of his tours. Scotland, particularly the Highlands, was largely unknown territory in the eighteenth century. The era of the tourist had not yet begun and Pennant's book was the first detailed account of this country and inspired many to follow and write of their experiences.

Falconry

Hawking was a popular form of hunting, especially in the Middle Ages, with the peregrine falcon being one of the prized birds. This bird was

Peregrine Falcon. (Roger Lee) Since protection measures were introduced their numbers have increased.

trained to gain height over an area where game, like partridge and grouse, were flushed out by beaters. It would then descend in its amazing stoop (swoop) and capture and kill its prey. There seems to have been a plentiful supply of falcons in Scotland and Atholl was no exception.

The coronation of King George IV took place in July 1821 and the 4th Duke was invited to attend and present a pair of falcons to the new King. This ceremony dated back to 1733, when the Atholl family acquired the Isle of Man and part of the contract was that they presented two falcons at the coronation of a monarch. By 1764 most of the Isle had been sold to the Crown but it was not until 1830 that the remaining properties were disposed of. As the Duke was unable to locate anyone on the Atholl estate able to capture and train the falcons, he engaged John Anderson, a falconer from Barrochan in Renfrew.[12] The Duke planned to travel south via Edinburgh and provided a seat on the outside of the mail coach for John Anderson and his falcons.

Anderson arrived in Atholl at the end of May and was taken up Glen Tilt by the Forest Lodge gamekeeper, Donald McIntyre and three assistants, where he was shown a crag where peregrines nested. Anderson duly captured three fine birds and set off for Dalnacardoch the next day, where more had been sighted. John Crerar met the falconer at Moulinearn after he had captured four more birds, saying he was "exceeding well pleased and that the two corries are the best for hawks that he knew".[13] The King indicated his desire that the falconer be attired in his traditional costume, and a Mr Beard provided a drawing for one, which he had produced from studying documents in the British Museum. Alexander Fraser, Lincoln's Inn, the Duke's London lawyer, wrote to him about this on 13 July 1821:

> On returning to chambers I found Mr Beard the Antiquarian waiting for me with a drawing for your Grace's Falconer made by him from documents found at the British Museum. Mr Beard is an amateur and volunteers services to do your Grace an act of civility on the request of the Heralds College. I hope it will suit you to be at home to receive the Antiquarian. He says there must be a lure, with bells hanging from a belt on the right side and that it is made of feathers and that on the left arm there must be a sort of crutch for the falcon to perch upon. As to the rest, his own drawings will best explain.
>
> He seems to think a Norman bonnett with an eagle's plume will be more appropriate than what he has drawn from the mss ...[14]

The coronation took place on Thursday 19 July and after the ceremony in Westminster Abbey, the Duke and other peers retired to Westminster Hall for the banquet, where the falcons were presented. The Duke's daughter, Lady Elizabeth Murray, attended the coronation and her journal contains a vivid description of the costume worn by the falconer:

On the day of the Coronation of George IV the Duke of Atholl as Lord of Man presented His Majesty with two falcons in Westminster Hall by which tenure His Grace held the Isle of Man. John Anderson (falconer) took care of the falcons and met His Grace in Edinburgh. He went with the falcons in the mail coach to London where he arrived with them in good health.

Anderson's dress was made by the most fashionable taylor and consisted of a green velvet jacket turned up with white gold lace, the Manx arms embroidered in the left arm, small cloathes of the same texture, green silk stockings, dress shoes and green rosettes, a black velvet hat with a plume of white ostrich feathers, a ruff round the neck, white leather gloves fringed with gold, a leather game bag and lure strapped over the shoulder.[15]

A few days later, the Duke with John Anderson, in full falconry costume, was again received by the King, this time at Carlton House. Anderson was presented with two silver bells engraved "George IV" and informed he was appointed Deputy Falconer of Scotland. When the King's state visit to Scotland took place the following year, Anderson attended and gave a demonstration of falcons catching pigeons before the King at Dalkeith.

Poachers

A major row broke out in July 1822, when the Duke interrogated a number of suspected poachers in Blair Castle. Donald McIntyre, the Forest Lodge keeper was well aware that they were persistent poachers and having seen one of them, Charles Campbell, fire at a deer the previous winter, went to the parish minister, the Rev. John Stewart, and asked him to prevail on one of his elders, whose son had been seen poaching, but to no avail. The son, and some others, were alleged to have killed a deer near the house of Robert Stewart in Auchgobhal, another of the accused. The Duke's Perth lawyer, George Condie, said there was insufficient evidence to convict the accused and

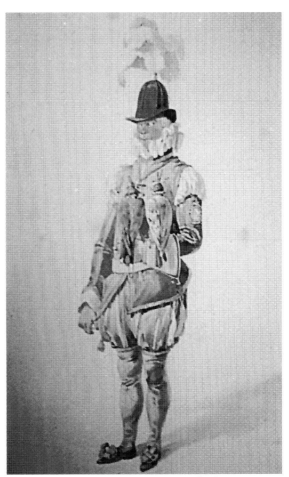
Sketch of a Falconer in the style of medieval costume recommended for the coronation of King George IV in 1821.

the case would not stand up in court. He considered it very probable the men were the culprits but advised the Duke not to bring an action, concluding that: "The people watching these rascals of poachers did not conceal themselves till they saw them fire at the deer. Killing of the hart could be referred to their oath, but I am satisfied that persons capable of doing such an illegal act will not hesitate to perjure themselves".[16]

Commonplace events in the glen are well covered in reports submitted by the factor and keepers, providing an insight into life there nearly two hundred years ago:

10 March 1799   Thomas Palliser, factor
There is no scarcity of either harts or hinds in the forest. John Crerar has been here since Wednesday. I went up to Forest Lodge with him, after which we looked into Glen Criny and Glen Mark, where we saw a great number of deer. The snow in many places there will not be off in the course of next summer, some of the wreaths are as high as this house.

One of Robertson's sons in Dalnagelsich [925 734] had a very narrow escape when out looking after the sheep near to the side of the Tilt; he heard a

A Peregrine Falcon like those required by the Duke of Atholl as tribute for the Isle of Man, at King George IV's coronation in 1821. (Roger Lee)

great noise; on looking up he saw a considerable quantity of snow comeing from the top of the hill, he got in below a rock and called his dog to come to him, but it refused, and was carried away by the snow into the river, and was lost. The snow rushed down with such violence into the river that it threw out to the opposite side several birch trees, a great deal of ice, and some trout, about fifty yards into the field behind the stables.[17]

Thomas Palliser was appointed factor to the Atholl estate in 1797 but had to resign ten years later because he "became deranged, presumably from an over-indulgence in spirits, and had to be removed from his position". He returned to his native Northumberland where he died in 1819.

26 May 1820   John Crerar, gamekeeper
Yesterday we went to Grueshill [Dunkeld] for the hawks. We got two young ones, very fine. I wrote to McIntyre and he has found two nests but has not taken the young out ...[18]

20 Jan 1822   John Crerar
I had a line from McIntyre on Friday last. He says that the two harts is far out in the forest and he mentioned that he thinks by the fine weather that the harts will be better than last year ... The carrion crows and magpies are pairing and the ravens were building last week ...[19]

30 March 1822   John Crerar
The hart with the large head of horns of 15 branches is in the wood behind Blairuachter and a very large parcel of sum hundred or so with him ...[20]

29 November 1822   John Crerar
I forgot to mention last week that McIntyre and his man took two speres and a rod from Braemar people killing black fish [out of season] from Lochen [Loch Tilt] top of Glen Tilt.[21]

13 July 1823   Donald McIntyre, Forest Lodge
This day I brought here two young eagles. One of them is the largest in all this country. This day there was a very large parcell of harts in the west corries of Glen Cranie ...[22]

Donald McIntyre, the Forest Lodge keeper, died on 9 March 1825, "having been perfectly collected and composed until his death". His final remarks were that no man had ever enjoyed life and occupation more than he and his last request was that he should be buried in a larch coffin.

A stone grouse butt, capped with turf.

29 October 1824   John Crerar, gamekeeper
I got the order yesterday for the eagle feathers. I happened to have mine by me which I gave to the Coach Office this day to go for Capt. James Murray as directed.[23]

12 November 1824   John Crerar
The warrender [rabbit warrener] has brought in here the other day seven pollcat, four house cats and one wild cat skins which is what he catched since 21 November last ...[24]

17 December 1824   John Crerar
Charles [his son] catched another potcher in Glenbanvie and Menzies had a long run after the other but got off from him ...[25]

6 April 1826   John Crerar
I looked at the several setts [butts] your Grace caused the mason to build for the purpose of shooting the harts crossing the glen which will I think be warm and convenient for good shott when passing ...[26]

Forest Lodge

Forest Lodge 933 741 dates from 1779 at the time when the 4th Duke was developing and enlarging his deer forests and requiring accommodation to make access to them more convenient. William Scrope made the following observations about the new lodge:

It is constructed without affectation of ornament and consists of two tenements united by a stone screen surrounded by stags' horns, and in which there is an archway for carriages to pass. One of these tenements serves for the lord of the forest and his friends and the other for his retinue.[27]

There were many visitors to the lodge during the shooting season and in September 1795, the Duchess and six ladies paid a visit to the Duke, staying for two nights. Duchess Marjory, Miss Woodford and little Lady Elizabeth Murray travelled in a phaeton, Lady Emilie, Miss Anne Knight and George Farquhar were in a buggy, while Lady Charlotte Murray and Miss Ogg, governess, travelled on horseback. They were accompanied by their servants and the eight mile journey from Blair Castle took two hours. A sumptuous dinner was served at five o' clock, while the evening was spent playing cards and dancing. An eyewitness recorded that "they romped, laughed and roared till fore in the morning". As there were only two bedrooms, one of which was occupied by the Duke and Duchess, accommodation was something of a problem. It seems the six ladies were packed into the second bedroom, where they slept two to a bed.

Next day, some of the ladies, dressed in "riding Jackets, Muslin Petticoats and each with a cudgel to lean upon" set off to walk to Loch Loch. After four miles they stopped at the bothy at Dail Chruineachd, "an empty hut, and rested on the floor, there being no seats, a quarter of an hour". After fording the Tilt with great difficulty, they

The original Forest Lodge in 1801 was very cramped and consisted of two buildings linked by an archway over the glen track. (J. Smith)

reached the loch after a two hour walk, when they had lunch.[28]

Forest Lodge was small and cramped, and could only accommodate the keepers and ghillies who attended the shooting parties, with great difficulty. The glen track passed beneath the archway which separated the buildings and this was as far as wheeled traffic could travel. Minor repairs were carried out to the lodge in 1810, when the thatched roof was mended and the exterior white-washed. A contemporary account described the lodge as being "all white washed and the roof is all pointed and the gravel is finished".[29]

To alleviate the accommodation problems, a bothy, 22 feet by 16 feet was built nearby to house servants and this was given some urgent attention as the Duke planned to let out the lodge and deer forest for the shooting season. Only a few years earlier he had leased some grouse moors but this was the first time a deer forest was to be let. The Duke's London lawyers, whom he consulted about this idea, were very sceptical, with one of them observing: "By letting a considerable part into sheep farming your Grace will receive more than double the return

which could be acquired by any other mode of letting the whole merely as a Forrest, and yet leave sufficient to maintain a suitable Herd of Deer to keep up and preserve the ancient and modern character of the Forrest".[30]

Fuel for heating and cooking purposes for the tenants in the lodge, was a prime essential, so a supply of peat was dug from a moss near the top of **Glen Craoinidh,** 911 737 above Clachglas. The cost of this to the estate in 1827 was as follows:[31]

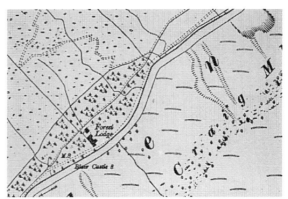

Extract from the 1900 edition of the Ordnance Survey map showing the location of Forest Lodge by the Tilt.

	£	s	d
Casting [cutting] at 1/6 a day for 16 people	1	4	0
Filling for 6 people		7	0
Leading [carting] at 1/3 a load 8 people and 69 loads	4	6	3
Stacking at 1/6 and 1/- a day 14 people for 14 days		16	6
Thatching [peat stacks] George Ritchie		8	0
Repairing peat road		16	6
	7	18	3

Realising that the condition of the lodge made it impossible to let out to wealthy shooting tenants, the Duke arranged for extensive alterations to be carried out in 1829 and 1830. Charles Sim, a Stanley builder was asked to tender for the job and regretted he was unable to meet the Duke on the appointed day because of a mishap earlier in the week:

> ... on my way home on Saturday last, when crossing the Tummel Ferry along with some herds and others, the rapidity of the current carried the boat beyond its landing place when I and some others were precipitated into the river but fortunately we got all safe out again altho' we received some little injury ...[32]

His estimate came to £149, which included repairing the dry stone south wall, and much underpinning of the old buildings. A more comprehensive plan was submitted in February 1830 by W.Mackenzie of Perth, under the heading, "Estimate for Forest Lodge exclusive of porch and renewing of Gray Slate roof with blue slates":[33]

Estimate for the probable expence of additions

	£	s	d
Mason Work	54	7	8
Carpenter and joiner Work	132	15	0
Plaster Work	30	18	4
Slater Work	22	8	0
Plumber Work	30	0	0
Bell hanging	7	0	0
	£277	9	0

The Duke of Buccleuch was one of the first tenants of Forest Lodge and he made further considerable alterations. One of them was to convert the area beneath the archway into a room called "the ladys' waiting room". Now the lodge contained a dining room, five bedrooms, a ladies' maids' room, servants' quarters and hall, pantry, kitchen, scullery larder and dairy. In addition there was a coal house, coach house for two carriages and a seven-stall stable.

In 1873 the accommodation was further extended when a house for the keeper was built to replace the bothy and a venison larder completed. At the end of the century it was described as being "a very unpretentious long low cottage, with servants' cottage and outhouses. Buildings are surrounded by a young and thriving

Ach Mhairc Mhoir 888 715 with a lint pool in the foreground, was the largest settlement in Glen Tilt.

plantation of trees of various kinds". Up to this period it had been single-storey but in 1907 it was extended yet again, with the addition of an upper floor, the coach house being turned into a garage, while the stables were converted into a house for the keeper. When the factor, John Forbes, paid a visit to the building site on 10 April 1907, he commented that there were nine builders plus labourers working there at the time. The east wing between the old dining room and adjoining bedroom would be ready for joisting in a few days and the part housing the new dining room and drawing room, shortly afterwards.

Bird's eye view of Forest Lodge as seen from the lower slopes of Carn Torcaidh.

Work was nearly completed by June when the factor gave a further progress report:

> ... the joiner would I think finish today in the East wing and round to Smoking room. The servants' rooms are well on also being lined (with wood) except one or two rooms. The painters have already given one or two coats of paint to all the guest rooms (woodwork) and varnished the woodwork of the stair, and as 4 extra painters are there this week they will very soon complete the painter work.[34]

Everything was ready for the 12 August and the start of the new season. Since that time no major structural alterations have been undertaken in the lodge.

Marble Lodge

Marble Lodge 899 717 was built in 1815 on the site of an old settlement called Inchgrennich, to provide additional accommodation for keepers and ghillies in the glen. Inchgrennich was once a settlement with about twelve acres set aside for crops, but it was deserted by around 1800. Many of the stones from the old houses were used to build a large enclosure, as well as the new lodge, which was named after the nearby quarry where the famous green Glen Tilt marble was hewn. Alterations followed in 1827 when a shed was erected to the rear to serve as a coach and peat house and one of the rooms was turned into a stable.

Marble Lodge was built in 1815 to afford more accommodation for keepers and ghillies.

Bothies

The Balaneasie Bothy 909 719 stands on the east bank of the Tilt, amidst the ruins of an old settlement of the same name. It was built in the nineteenth century when the settlement was cleared and is now used for outdoor recreational purposes. Six miles upstream, at the confluence of the Tilt and An Lochain, are the remains of the **Dail a' Chruineachd Bothy** 980 783, now very overgrown with grass and nettles. This was built over a three-week period in 1792 by eight men, with John Stewart mason, at Bridge of Tilt and James Stewart

The Balaneasie Bothy beside the Tilt.

being paid one shilling and eight pence a day, with others at a shilling a day. The masons' bill amounted to £7.9.4 along with another charge for "pulling, leading and thatching with heather, £2.18.0".[35] At about 3 pm on 9 October 1861, Queen Victoria, Prince Albert and their entourage stopped here for a picnic lunch on their return journey from Dalwhinnie and Blair

Castle to Balmoral, on what was to be their last expedition together.

The area of level ground on the east side of the river was the site of a royal feast in 1529, when King James V of Scotland, accompanied by his mother, Queen Margaret and the Pope's ambassador, stayed there for three days to go on a royal hunt and be entertained. John, the 3rd

Four of the 28 corries in the Beinn a' Ghlo mountain range.

Earl of Atholl was keen to demonstrate his power and wealth by entertaining his guests in as extravagant a manner as they would have received in Edinburgh. At great expense he built a temporary wooden palace with glazed windows and rich furnishings where his guests ate a sumptuous banquet. The Earl has also assembled hundreds of his men to form an immense circle and herd the deer, over a period of days towards the site of the hunt. This whole exercise was said to have cost the Earl £1,000 a day, a staggering fortune in those times. During the tinchel two hundred deer, a wolf, a fox and several wild cats were killed.

BEINN A' GHLO FOREST

This deer forest covers the Beinn a' Ghlo mountain range on the east side of Glen Tilt and contains four mountains over 3,000 feet. They are: **Carn Liath** (3,169 feet) 936 698; **Braigh Coire Chruinn-bhalgain** (3,302 feet) 949 725; **Airgiod Bheinn** (3,448 feet) 962 720; and **Carn nan Gabhar** (3,669 feet) 971 733. Within this range are twenty eight corries whose names were recorded in "The Highlander" of February 1877. Charles Ferguson and the Durness Free Church minister discussed them with an old man called James Mackenzie in the 1830s and wrote down the names of the corries which "nestle among the vast so-called progeny of the great mountains".

Charles Pirie has been the Tilt, Tarf and Beinn a' Ghlo keeper for the past 3 years. (Roger Lee) Before that he was keeper at Kindrochet Lodge from 1970.

Coireachan Beinn A' Ghlo

Coire Ghlo		corrie of the mist
Choinnich	928 703	mossy corrie
Chromaltan	932 714	corrie of crooked streamlet
nan Dearcag		corrie of the blaeberry
Ghlas		grey corrie
Odhar		dun corrie
Fhiann	934 726	Fingalian corrie
Thorcaidh	938 735	wild boar's corrie
Chailleach	951 752	corrie of the old woman
Ghlas Leathad	962 740	corrie of the grey slope
Chaisteal	969 744	castle corrie
Rainich	958 755	ferny corrie
Buidh Mor	953 740	big yellow corrie
Buidh Beag	943 730	little yellow corrie
Chuinidh Mor		corrie of the big coin
Chuinidh Beag		corrie of the little coin
Alltan 'ic Mhuirich	965 754	corrie of the little stream of MacMurdoch
Direadh ri Bruthach		climbing the brae corrie
Breac	982 755	speckled corrie
n' Alltan Deirg	964 763	corrie of the little red stream
na Mearach	977 745	corrie of branches
Cas Fhiachlach	975 736	corrie of gnashing teeth
nan Cisteachan	977 729	corrie of the chest
Laggan	968 722	corrie of little hollow
Crom	931 717	bent corrie
Chruinnbhalgan	947 724	little round bag corrie
na Saobhaidh	942 764	corrie of fox's den
Chleirich		corrie of the cleric

Grid references are given to those corries located on the appropriate Ordnance Survey maps, based on the 6" edition for 1900. Exact locations of eight of the twenty eight have yet to be made.

86

ATHOLL DEER FORESTS
WEST HAND • BRUAR • CLUNES • KINDROCHET

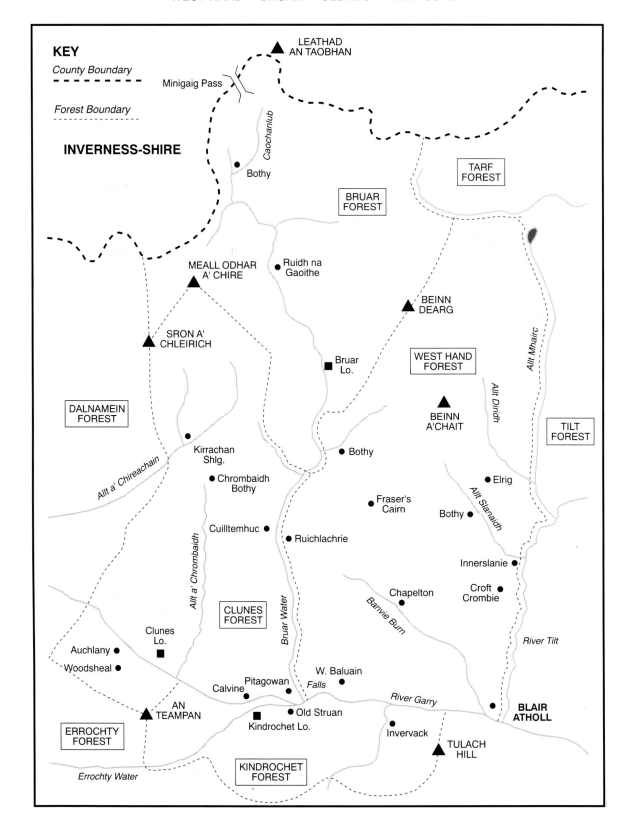

KEY

County Boundary

Forest Boundary

INVERNESS-SHIRE

LEATHAD AN TAOBHAN

Minigaig Pass

Caochanlub

● Bothy

TARF FOREST

BRUAR FOREST

MEALL ODHAR A' CHIRE

● Ruidh na Gaoithe

BEINN DEARG

SRON A' CHLEIRICH

Bruar Lo.

WEST HAND FOREST

BEINN A'CHAIT

DALNAMEIN FOREST

Allt Mhairc

Allt Diridh

TILT FOREST

Kirrachan Shlg.

Allt a' Chireachain

● Bothy

● Elrig

● Chrombaidh Bothy

Fraser's Cairn

Bothy ●

Allt Slanaidh

Cuilltemhuc ●

● Ruichlachrie

Allt a' Chrombaidh

Innerslanie ●

CLUNES FOREST

Bruar Water

Chapelton

Croft Crombie ●

Banvie Burn

River Tilt

Clunes Lo.

Auchlany ●

Woodsheal ●

W. Baluain

Calvine ● Pitagowan ●

Falls

River Garry

BLAIR ATHOLL

AN TEAMPAN

Old Struan ●

Invervack ●

ERROCHTY FOREST

Kindrochet Lo.

TULACH HILL

KINDROCHET FOREST

Errochty Water

WEST HAND FOREST

This forest covers the ground immediately to the north of Blair Castle and is sometimes called the Castle Beat. Being the nearest deer forest to the family residence, it was usually set aside for the Duke, his friends and guests. It centres on **Beinn a' Chait** (hill of cats) 865 749, which at 2,921 feet misses being classed as a Munro by only a few feet. Though nearly exterminated, wild cats still inhabit the lonely and inhospitable terrain of this mountain. Gleann Mhairc forms the eastern boundary of the forest, while to the west it cuts across **Beinn Dearg** (red hill) 853 777 and then proceeds down Bruar Water to the Garry.

A Family of Wildcats. (Roger Lee) During the 1884/85 shooting season, 159 were shot in the Atholl forests.

In *Deer and Deer Forests of Scotland,* McConnachie described this forest in the 1920s thus:

> The mountains in the forest are somewhat steep and generally rocky; they present many corries which require to be stalked with care. There is much succulent pasture, particularly in Gleann Mhairc and Gleann Diridh, with abundance of moss-crop. The low-ground shooting is very good, the bag including grouse, black game, duck, snipe, pheasants, partridges, hares and rabbits. The Garry and the Tilt are both good for a few salmon, and trout streams are numerous. There are several eagles' eyries, and ravens also breed in the forest; the badger too has been seen.

Gleann Diridh (ascending glen) 883 721, locally known as "the half glen" was developed as a nursery for deer in 1738, when the Duke decreed that "no person shall enter the nursery except when the forester is present". This site remains so to this day as hundreds of hinds with their calves are to be found here each spring. There has always been an abundance of deer in this forest as John Crerar reported in 1795:

> In Glen Banvie and above Croftcrombie as at near a calculation as I could reckon, there were no less

than two thousand deer, and four hundred of that number harts.[1]

Croft Crombie 876 689 lies on the north or "sunny side" of Glen Tilt, on open hillside which in 1780 contained 155 acres of cultivable ground. It consisted of thirteen buildings with two corn drying kilns and became deserted in 1789 when the area was turned over to cattle grazing.

Poaching

Being so close to human habitation and main roads, the West Hand deer forest was a favourite haunt for poaching. In 1805 a Donald Macbeath was living in **Ruichlachrie** (stony shieling) 819 706, a good croft on the east bank of the Bruar Water, which was capable of carrying at least thirty sheep and some cows. Macbeath reported having seen Peter Robertson, a weaver in Bridge of Bruar, Alex Robertson and Duncan Stewart, also weavers, along with Archibald McGillivrie, a tailor, all living in Invervack, carrying guns, save for McGillivrie, who had a stick. As Macbeath approached, asking them if they had authority to shoot in the forest, Alex Robertson pointed his gun at him, telling him to "stand back". Undaunted, Macbeath came closer and was then told that "he might take his chance". Peter Robertson was in possession of a musket and was a private in Captain John Stewart's Company of the Atholl Battalion, while Duncan Stewart had a single-barrelled fowling piece. As no violence had been committed and no deer shot, the alleged poaching case was dropped.[2]

Ten years later, in January 1815, John Stewart, the estate overseer, reported seeing two men firing at a deer near Craig Urrard. He followed the traces of blood to Pitagowan, then on to a house in Lambton occupied by a cottar (holder of a small piece of land, in return for services, often labouring) called James McLaren. Lambton was also known as Wester Baluain and the tenant at this time was Alex Gow. John Stewart obtained a search warrant but when McLaren's wife answered the door she denied any knowledge of her husband's whereabouts. Stewart, the overseer, did not believe her and, "not satisfied with her answer, I went through the house and found a man hiding behind a bed with his gun and a new-killed deer. I also found 2 haunches of venison and apprehended the gun and the plunder."[3]

The factor was surprised that Alex Gow had encouraged poaching "as it was impossible that McLaren can be going out without Gow's knowledge" and he too was bound over to appear in court. Wester Baluain seems to have been a

Pitagowan in 1860 - a typical Highland hamlet of houses and outbuildings scattered over a wide area. Traces of blood in the snow from a deer killed by poachers, were tracked here in 1815.

hot-bed of poachers, as, a few years earlier another tenant, Robert Stewart, had been warned to leave the district for the same reason. Reporting to the Duke, John Crerar wrote that:

> I went to Blair last week upon hearing that the people were shooting the deer about Craig Urrard, and upon enquiry found that Robert Stewart, late lint miller at the far end of Blairuachter, and now in Lambton, with his sons and a smith in Strowan, were the people that was shooting them, and by information these people has not been idol for sum time past. As to venison being found, there was no search made, as when the aggressors' friends found that people was speaking about them, their friends sent word to them to put it out of the way or I should have got a warrant and search'd as Moon traced the horse foot marks to Stewart's door from where they took the deer up ... Stewart should be remov'd; it would keep others in these towns from going out with guns.[4]

Despite repeated warnings Stewart refused to leave and when finally ordered to go within 48 hours, still paid no attention. A sheriff's "Warrand of Ejection" was therefore issued for immediate execution with the instructions that, "after all his household furniture is thrown out, lock the doors and keep the keys ..."

Also around this time, Donald Robertson, a 29-year-old Glen Tilt shepherd was on Beinn a' Chait with John Walker, when he saw a man take a shot at a deer. On investigating the incident they met William Gordon, a foxhunter from Badenoch, who was carrying a gun and accompanied by two other men with two greyhounds, two foxhounds and several terriers. They claimed to have been clearing out a den of foxes and Gordon denied having shot at any deer. He promised to leave immediately but made out he had killed foxes there before, without any problems. Since Robertson could not swear absolutely that Gordon was the man who had fired, the matter was dropped.[5] Each of the forests had its own foxhunter and in 1824, a total of 26 foxes, including 19 young ones, were killed in Glen Tilt.[6]

Foxes were hunted ruthlessly in the Atholl forests. (Roger Lee) 125 were killed in 1884/85.

In February 1830 several of Charles MacGregor's sub tenants were spotted leaving the wood above the Cults, part of the castle parkland, where two deer had been killed the previous night. Once again the keepers followed the traces of blood in the snow, this time to Woodend.[7] By the time a search warrant had been obtained, a further heavy fall of snow obliterated all tracks and traces and despite searching all the houses between Woodend and Calvine as well as Invervack, across the Garry, where the poachers were thought to live, no trace of anything was found.[8]

During the 1890s, John Stewart, a notable Atholl Highlander and gamekeeper retired to Ruichlachrie for the last eight years of his life. He was born in Glen Fincastle and entered the service of the 6th Duke of Atholl as a gamekeeper. After spending a few years at Fealar, he was in charge of the Glen Tilt beats for 33 years, based at Clachglas. He was reckoned to have been one of the best deer stalkers of his time and when Queen Victoria passed through the glen on her way to Balmoral in 1861, he was one of the Atholl hillmen who escorted her to Bynack Lodge on Deeside. For this he was presented with an artist's proof of the watercolour by Carl Haag entitled "The Fording of the Poll Tarff". In early life he was an athlete of some note and a great performer of Highland reels. He was an Atholl Highlander for 49 years, with the reputation of having never missed a parade. He married, had three sons and five daughters and during his final years, built the mile-long track from the Nine Mile Drive to Ruichlachrie.[9] It ceased being run as a small farm in 1939 when the last tenant went off to fight in the Second World War and although the tenant survived, he did not return to the farm.

Bothies

There are two bothies in this forest. The **Allt Sheicheachan Bothy** (burn of the hides) 835 737 was built in 1881 and is 5¼ miles along the West Hand track from Blair Castle. It consists of a room and a two-stall stable and is now maintained by the Scottish Mountain Bothies Association as a haven for walkers and climbers. The track to it was completed in 1882. The other bothy is located just beyond the four-mile milestone beside **Allt Slanaidh** 867 718 where a wooden carriage shelter was erected in 1891. This is now used as a refuge and lunch hut for shooting parties. Until recently the track terminated here but has since been extended to pass round the base of Beinn a'Chait as far as Allt Sheicheachan and then downstream to link up with the West Hand track.

The Allt Sheicheachan Bothy 5¼ miles from Blair Castle, with the new track to Allt Slanaidh in the background.

Lord Glenlyon's Epic Ride

When Lord Glenlyon (afterwards the 6th Duke of Atholl), was courting Miss Anne Home Drummond of Blair Drummond in south-west Perthshire, they wrote to each other almost every

George, 6th Duke of Atholl in 1860. He succeeded to the title in 1846 and died in January 1864.

A milestone on the Nine Mile Drive indicates the distance covered and that remaining. The Drive starts from Blair Castle and runs in a circle through the lower part of the West Hand forest by the Falls of Bruar and returns by Glen Banvie to the Castle.

pretty near to us, but we could not see them. The mist then cleared for a little and we found we had in the face of Glen Tilt a magnificent herd of at least two thousand deer. We were above them and my groom on horseback below them to put them up to us again which he accomplished. They came stringing out at last past us within about 30 yards. I then let fly at them, my hands were so horribly numbed by the cold rain that I could not shoot as well as I do usually. I however brought down three fine beasts, 15 St. 13 St. and 12 St. 10½lbs. After this I got on my horse and rode home ...[10]

This arduous ride by Lord Glenlyon, followed by a gruelling deer stalk, cannot have failed to impress Miss Home Drummond with his great endurance, stamina, love and thrill of the "chase" along with an ability to shoot stags under very adverse conditions.

day. In a letter dated 17 September 1839, just over a month before their wedding, he tells her how he rode one day from Blair Drummond at 4 am, reached Dunblane by daylight and arrived in Crieff after two and a quarter hours. After a further two and a half hours he breakfasted in Dunkeld, having arrived there about 9 am. He left after half an hour, reaching Blair Castle at 11.25 am:

> I then put on my kilt and mounting a fresh horse I proceeded 9 miles further to where I was to meet the keepers. [the nine-mile stone at **Allt na Maraig** 943 750] I came up to them a little before 1 o'clock so that you see I accomplished the 74 miles in rather a short period and without feeling as if I had ridden any distance. The instant I got off my horse, down came the rain in torrents. The wind was easterly and bitterly cold. In less than a quarter of an hour we were thoroughly drenched and as we had to allow the men we had to send round the deer, time to do so, we had to sit shivering for about half an hour. The mist then came on very thick and the deer galloped down

Sandy Reid has been a keeper for 35 years, starting at Forest Lodge and has been the head keeper on the Atholl Estate for the past 17 years. (Roger Lee)

Fraser's Cairn, where two poachers in Glen Tarf were instructed by the Witch of Beinn a' Ghlo to place a "fat hart" on the first Monday of every month. (Captain Drummond of Megginch)

Gable end of a bothy in Ruidh Sron nan Dias (Seven Shielings), where a refuge hut was built in the 19th century.

A painting entitled "At the Tarf" shows a shooting party in 1856 beside a temporary wooden bridge resting on the buttresses of the old bridge.   (William Evans)

A group of sportsmen in Atholl in 1856. Left to right: Colonel Leith Hay of the 93rd Highlanders; Lieutenant Alexander Stewart and William Evans of Eton, the painter of a number of stalking and castle scenes which appear in this book.

BRUAR FOREST

Glen Bruar is reckoned to be classic ground for the deer stalker and stretches from the Inverness county boundary to **Allt a' Chaise** (cheese burn) 823 726 two miles south of Bruar Lodge, which William Scrope made his headquarters for a number of years. In his first ascent of Beinn Dearg he found the summit "strewed over with the bones of calves (fawns), lambs and moorfowl, which had fallen a prey to the fox, wild cat or eagle". The original lodge was situated nearly two miles further up the glen, where extensive ruins are all that remain of it, sited on the old shieling called **Ruidh na Gaoithe** (windy shieling) 824 783.

A large ruin, measuring 70 feet by 10 feet , which was the site of the first Bruar Lodge, below Creag na h-Iolair Mhor.

The new lodge, first called **Cabar Feith**, (deer's antler) 832 761 was built in 1789 on its present site to replace the old one which was too small. It comprised of a parlour, two bedrooms, gun room, servants' hall and bedroom, kitchen and pantry, forming three sides of a courtyard. A keeper's cottage, stable and byre were adjacent but detached.[1] As with all buildings so exposed to the elements in these remote glens, it was in need of constant maintenance, with major repairs being called for by 1810. The gable end of the stable wall had collapsed, along with part of the back wall and the dog kennel was in disrepair also. It was estimated that the cost of rebuilding the damaged gable and wall, along with re-thatching the kennel would be £6.[2]

William Scrope

In his early days in Atholl, Scrope cast covetous eyes on Forest Lodge in Glen Tilt but admitted he was unable to compare it with Bruar and thought anyway that the grouse shooting there would be inferior to Bruar. He also considered the rent too expensive. During the second year

of his tenancy in 1823, the estate made alterations and improvements to Bruar Lodge. Scrope proposed that he would paint or paper the two main rooms and, "when that is done" he wrote, "Miss Knight must not laugh at me if I hold it up as a rival to Forest Lodge".[3] Perhaps this is an indication that Scrope was determined on making Bruar the best lodge in Atholl. Miss Mary Anne Knight was a cousin and companion of Duchess Marjory, second wife of the 4th Duke, who lived with the family at Blair Castle.

Scrope was dissatisfied with the estate's repairs, writing to the Duke on 6 August 1823, complaining that Menzies had pulled down the milk house, "which was a great convenience to me - at least it was standing when I took possession and has now disappeared". He maintained that the repairs had not been carried out according to the Duke's instructions, "but with some trouble on my part, they seem to be at length in progress" he concluded.[4]

In his book, *Days of Deer Stalking,* Scrope gives a vivid description of Bruar Lodge as he found it at the start of his tenancy:

> At the right entrance of the pass, the little white and lonely dwelling called Bruar Lodge, lies a mere speck beneath it. It consists of two small tenements, facing each other, encompassed by a wall, so as to form a small court between them: one of these buildings serves for the master, and the other for his servants. There is, besides, a lodging place for two hill men, rather frail in structure, and a dog kennel of the same picturesque character. Close by stands a black stack of peats ...

Sketch of Bruar Lodge in 1860.

Descriptions of the glen from letters and reports give a close feel of life there in the nineteenth century:

5 April 1801 Thomas Palliser, factor
The weather was uncommonly fine when I was at

Blair, rather too hot. The deer from that circumstance was all out on the high hills. On Thursday I was at the head of Glen Tilt and on Friday at the head of Glen Bruar, from both of which places I saw a great many fine deer.[5]

Minigaig Fatality

The dangers of travel in winter in the hills were dramatically described in one of John Crerar's reports, which tells of a fatality on the Minigaig road, the old route to the north, which passed up Glen Bruar to the summit at the county march at a height of 2,745 feet, before descending to Speyside:

> 14 November 1823 John Crerar, gamekeeper
> The Weather is so good. Yesterday two weeks was the stormy day five women and three men took the Minigaig road. One of the women gave up upon the hill and one of the men being stout took her upon his back and she died unknown upon his back. The other was obliged to leave her to get on to a bothie beyond the march to save sum of the other women who with difficulty got to the bothie.[6]

Just before the start of the 1823 season, Scrope wrote to John Crerar enquiring whether the estate would supply various household items such as "sheets, towels, table cloths etc" and also whether he would receive "the usual common cottage furniture such as plates, tea things, knives and forks, tureens, grid irons and tell me what accommodation there is for horses".[7]

When the Duke read the letter, he disliked the inference that the estate was expected to supply household items and showed his displeasure by refuting this in the reply he dispatched by return. Only four days later, Scrope answered thus:

> I fear I must have expressed myself different from my intentions. My meaning was to ascertain that articles could be conveniently sent from Blair Atholl in order that my servant might not get duplicates and it was far from my intention to occasion any trouble or inconvenience of any sort. I am sufficiently flattered by being admitted as a tenant so near to Blair.[8]

By the following year Scrope was held in high esteem by the Duke, so much so, that he was able to ask to be made "Chief Forester" and promised to improve Bruar Lodge considerably, saying that it would be kept well aired and available for the Duke to sleep there rather than having the usual early start from Blair Castle. Scrope indicated his readiness to build a wooden coach-house and dog kennel, "put the place in good order" and have deer-hounds for the Duke's use whenever required.[9]

Deer-hounds and a pup, drawn by Sir Edwin and Thomas Landseer to illustrate "The Art of Deer Stalking" by William Scrope.

Servant Problems

It appears that Scrope had problems in recruiting staff for the lodge and was not happy with the herd he had employed. In 1825 he therefore sought the help of John Crerar, "to look out for me for an honest, active and steady herd to be put in Glen Bruar. He should be married and come from a distant quarter". Crerar recommended a man called Maclaren, so Scrope wrote to the factor on 16 April, asking for him to be engaged:

> ... Crerar tells me he has seen a married man that will do for me as a resident at Glen Bruar. His wages seem high - that is twelve pounds, a cow, two pecks of meal and his peats for a year's service. He has a good character. If therefore you think he will do for me, I should be much obliged to you to engage him. He must likewise lodge as he can - for his wife must sleep in the room with the other maids - I mean when my family is there. The Duke spoke about a single man who would have come much cheaper, but I am convinced it is out of nature for an unmarried man to remain in so lonely a place and do his duty ...[10]

At the same time, Scrope wrote to the Duke to keep him informed, commenting that although he was much the dearest, he felt sure he would "answer best". He also hoped that the new herd "would prove to be more attentive to his duties than the former one".[11] It was not until the first winter that the new herd, Maclaren, became dissatisfied and began complaining that peats cast at Ruichlachrie had not been delivered to the lodge and he therefore could not remain there throughout the winter. The Duke was most indignant about his request to move down the glen to Ruichlachrie "as it is very important for the preservation of the forest that he should be in the Lodge".[12] Scrope observed that Maclaren would welcome any excuse to live lower down the glen in winter.

Reporting on this, the factor wrote to Scrope on 18 December 1825 refuting the claim made by Maclaren that insufficient stocks of peat and hay had been sent up to the lodge to permit him to stay there. He insisted that there were two months' supply of peat and sufficient hay to feed two cows during the winter. "It is likely that the man would be glad of any excuse to get away from Bruar to Riechlachrie", he concluded.

Deer-Hounds

Having promised the Duke that deer-hounds would be available for his use at any time, Scrope was anxious to develop a small pack and Charles Crerar commented to his father, John, in July 1826 that: "Mr Scrope's young dog is offering well and will be a good one and mores the pity there is no more of them. The other young dog of George's own breeding I am afraid will never be good for anything".[13]

A few days later Scrope wrote to the Duke informing him of his progress:

> ... Crerar is hard at work breaking in the dogs. He says he has only two tolerable ones except that bred from my dog which is the best of all. Macpherson killed one the other day by letting some wood fall accidentally on him in unloading a cart. Ritchie it seems gave him another puppy got by my dog, which he had no business to do. It is very handsome and promises to be excellent.[14]

Scrope was a first-rate rifle shot and in only his second season in Atholl, between 15 August and 14 October, he killed 26 brace of grouse; 36 stags; 5 hinds; 15 partridges and 12 hares. John Forbes, an Atholl ponyman, was much admired by Scrope. He was nicknamed Curly (after his hair) and for twenty years looked after the hill ponies which brought the deer down the glen. He knew every part of the forest and could be directed to find a dead deer even though it might be lying up to twenty miles away. He died in the late 1820s.

Poaching

Despite the apparent remoteness of Glen Bruar it had its share of poachers. In January 1828 one of the Bruar keepers was on a hilltop between Glen Bruar and the Kirrachan Shieling to the west, when the mist cleared and he spied a man, about half a mile away, carrying something on his back. The keeper set off in pursuit and the man, seeing him gaining ground, dropped his sack and made good his escape in the mist. The sack contained the forequarters of a young stag. Next morning the keeper went over to Chapelton in Glen Banvie where he saw the same man shooting a deer, and although the keeper again pursued him, the poacher made his way across the Bruar Water and again escaped.[15]

A few days later, Frederick Graham, the factor commented on this incident:

> ... frequently when the evidence of the gamekeeper has promised to be most conclusive from the verbal and written reports, it has been found totally defective in the course of the proceedings in Perth.
>
> The penalty is so trifling and the person so poor that whether they can pay or not, the punishment is inadequate to the temptation. If they cannot pay, they must be alienated during imprisonment and the expence of the prosecution is increased. If they can pay, they do so easily out of the game.[16]

This incident illustrates the difficulties that estates encountered in providing enough proof to convict poachers when taken to court. In another example, two alleged poachers were caught in Glen Bruar and their case brought before two Justices of the Peace in Blair Atholl on 2 May 1845. W. Robertson from Glen Bruar and Angus Macdonald in Cuilltemhuc, also in Glen Bruar, were accused of "trespassing in pursuit of deer on or about 15 March 1845", and both said they

Cuilltemhuc, the home of Angus Macdonald, who, when accused of poaching in Glen Bruar, said he was shooting foxes.

were not guilty. A gamekeeper, John Stewart, swore from the witness stand that he saw two tracks in the snow, which he followed and saw three men leaving Bruar Lodge and crossing to the opposite bank of the river. He went to the lodge, where after a few minutes, W. Robertson and Charles Fraser appeared, with Robertson carrying a gun. The men maintained they had been following a fox and had not been shooting deer. Once again the case was inconclusive, because although the men were known poachers, there was no proof of them having fired at, let alone having killed a deer.[17]

Bruar Lodge Enlarged

During the 1838 season, Lord Glenlyon occupied Bruar Lodge and made plans for extending it. William Burn, an Edinburgh architect, at 131 George Street submitted plans "for such additions and alterations as would appear necessary for your accommodation".[18] However, it appears that in that year the Duke of Buccleuch terminated his lease of Glen Tilt, so Lord Glenlyon changed his mind and took up quarters at Forest Lodge instead. Nevertheless the plans to extend Bruar Lodge went ahead and the old building was considerably enlarged by the two original buildings, one for the tenant and the other for servants, being joined up, while a cart shed, slaughter house, gig house and a much

larger stable were added on at the east end. Elsewhere another bedroom and extra servants' quarters were built round a small courtyard. In 1888 further alterations were carried out to complete the lodge as we know it today and a small shelter plantation was established above the lodge in 1893.

Because of the services he rendered to the Duke, Scrope was allowed to lease Bruar Lodge rent free. On his departure in 1833 it was advertised to let for a rent of £200 a year. Tenants were restricted to 15 stags in a season and were on no account to "stalk hunt and shoot deer when the wind is from the north".

In 1846 it was advertised as having first-rate shooting for three guns and "there is a lodge on the ground, comfortably furnished".[19] By 1870 the yearly rent was £700, with the tenant paying the keeper's wages, a proportion of the Poor Rates, along with maintenance of the house and furniture during his absence. By this time the forest extended to nearly 12,000 acres, of which 3,000 were cleared of sheep and most important for the tenant, there were no restrictions on the number of deer they were allowed to shoot. In 1884/85 the following were shot in the Glen Bruar forest: stag 40; hind 3; grouse 702 brace; ptarmigan 30; snipe 5; wild fowl 7; plover 10; white hare 21; fox 1; weasel 4; hoodie crow 8; hawk 4; raven 1; peregrine falcon 2.

By this time the forest had been divided up into thirteen clearly defined beats as follows:[20]

1. House — best for grouse and hares
2. Allt a' Chaise (cheese burn) — good for grouse
3. Sron na Faicheachan — good for grouse
4. Feith Gorm Ailleag — good for deer and grouse
5. South Gaick
6. North Gaick
7. Uchd a' Chlarsair — good for grouse
8. Allt Damh Dubh (black ox burn) — good for grouse
9. Feith Odhar Mhor — good for grouse
10. Feidh Odhar Beag
11. Forest Beat
12. Flat Beat
13. The Glen — best for ptarmigan and deer

Grazing

Glen Bruar was extensively grazed in earlier times as is shown in a rental for 1707, when James Stewart from Clunes was given authority to:

Pasture and grass such cattle thereon as he shall think fit restricting always the said cattle to the number of 400, he entering to the grassings against the first of May next and leaving them void against the 29th of September ...[21]

His rent was set at 100 merks (£5.11.1 Sterling) yearly and also a "sufficient fat cow".

At the head of the glen and high up on the Grampian plateau, two miles from the county march with Inverness-shire are the remains of a solitary shieling bothy, standing at 2,275 feet above sea level, at the confluence of two streams. This shieling, which was the highest recorded in Atholl, was called **Caochan Lub** (meandering stream) 810 821.

Aeneas Macpherson from Killihuntly in Badenoch, being in need of summer pasture, wrote to the Marquis of Atholl on 24 June 1696:

Being straitened for want of hill grass, I by this letter make my address and seek the liberties of graisseing from your land any place lest prejudicial to your Lordship's interest and most convenient for me. I am content to pay yearly and I shall not stay above a fortnight, nor go to it before July.[22]

His request was granted and he obtained a warrant "to pasture and grass my goods in his Grace's shiell called Krichanaloup [Caochan Lub] lying to the north side of Glen Bruar". But in 1704 when the factor made a check of the shieling tenants, he was apparently surprised to discover that Aeneas Macpherson was pasturing far too many cattle in this remote place. The factor's memo of 22 September records the details:

Killiehuntly shealls in the sheallings of Caochannaluib and Madhuy, which are about a

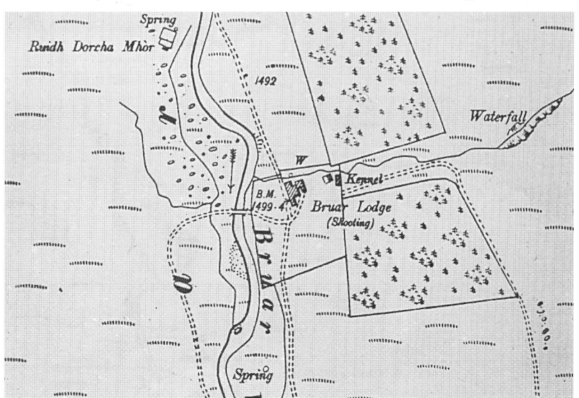

Extract from the 1900 edition of the Ordnance Survey map showing Bruar Lodge beside Bruar Water.

Ian McCulloch, the present Glen Bruar keeper. (Roger Lee)

Bowman [cattle man] who sheall thereon likewise and that this year he will have about 57 head of cattle. It is informed that he kills a great many deer in the forest having hired of late the best stalker in the two counties.[23]

Steps were immediately taken to counter this, with Aeneas agreeing to reduce the number of cattle to between 30 and 40 and getting rid of the stalker, under a penalty of 500 merks (£27.15.6 Sterling) for any further contravention. He further agreed that "if any of my men shall be found guilty of killing deer within His Grace's forest, that I shall bring them to any of His Grace's Courts ..."

At the same time, Aeneas was complaining about "mismanagement and trespass" of the Duke of Gordon's foresters in Badenoch, which, he said, "is destroying Atholl Forests where they march together" and asked the Duke to investigate. Instead the Duke appointed Aeneas to be his gamekeeper in that area, allowing him to kill two deer yearly for his own use, as payment for this duty.

It was the old Minigaig Pass route through the Grampians from Blair Atholl to Ruthven in Badenoch that brought prosperity to Glen Bruar and along its twelve mile length there were at one time a number of settlements and shielings. However, the coming of General Wade's military road through Drumochter in 1728 deprived the glen of its main source of income and hastened its population decline. Nowadays the lower part is somewhat bleak and uncompromising and apart from the gamekeeper and his wife living at Bruar Lodge, the glen is empty for much of the year.

mile distant which two places being very prejudicial to the deer, they being the very nursery of them and which the harts ordinarily frequent till the time of them copuling with the hinds.

It is said he keeps a great many cattle there not only in his own name but under the name of

CLUNES AND KINDROCHET FORESTS

In his book *Deer & Deer Forests of Scotland* published in 1922, Alex McConnachie gives a comprehensive description of the Clunes forest as it was over seventy years ago:

> Clunes Lodge is delightfully situated on the Garry about two miles north-west of Struan station. The forest ground is drained by Allt a' Chire Mhoir and Allt a' Chire Bhig, two burns which form the Allt a' Chireachain. Leac Liath (1788 feet) is near the centre of the ground.
>
> Fully a square mile of woodland is open for the deer. The forest ground is good for a bag of twenty stags; average, clean, 14½st.; the class of heads is also good. Ten hinds are shot in winter. The south-west wind is the best, and the north the worst, for the forest.
>
> The moor is good for over 1000 brace of grouse. The bag also includes a few roe deer, partridges, black game, plover and snipe. Golden plover, at one time very plentiful, are now rather scarce. There is no lack of trouting streams and the Garry yields a number of salmon.
>
> Near the head of Gleann Chrombaidh there is a bothy with stable for the convenience of stalkers. The pasture is excellent and the supply of moss crop very plentiful.

The Clunes forest is one of the smaller in Atholl, stretching from the Bruar Water and Allt

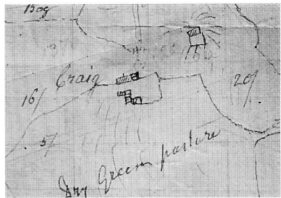

A 1790 plan by James Stobie of the settlement of Craig in the Clunes forest.

a' Chaise in the east to Sron a' Chleirich in the west. It also crosses the River Garry to the south, taking in the lands of Woodsheal and Auchlany, as far as the watershed with Glen Errochty.

In 1712, Donald Robertson, younger son of Robertson of Kincraigie (in Glenfender) was appointed to be in charge of the Clunes Wood and was "allowed as much timber yearly out of the Wood as will repair and uphold the biggings

An aerial view of Craig showing the footings of several deserted buildings and a large enclosure.

[buildings] on Clunebeg [his home] and he divides the sneddings [lopped branches] amongst the tennents of the property which may be sned on all occasions except in the months of March, April and May yearly".[1]

A few years later, William Murray was appointed gamekeeper with powers to exact a fine of forty shillings Scots for each lowland ox found pasturing there. Failure to meet this fine resulted in the livestock being impounded until the matter was settled.

John Crerar's son, Charles, was in the Clunes area in July 1826 and what he saw was included in his father's next report to the Duke:

> Charles on Thursday was in the Kirrachan next Glen Bruar. He seed five broods [of grouse] next Glen Bruar side from seven to eight in each ... He saw forty hart the morning he went to Kirrachan up behind the wood with large heads and looked very full and fatt. No hinds with them ...[2]

Kirrachan Shieling

The **Kirrachan Shieling** (shieling of the combs) 793 737 has still the remains of more than twenty buildings scattered around the confluence of two streams, Allt a' Chire Mhoir and Allt a' Chire Bhig, at the south end of a 2,500 acre expanse of moorland. This area was feued as their shieling, to the Stewart lairds of Shierglas and Strathgarry

in 1708. By 1800 only one bothy, which was occupied by a herd for these two lairds, remained standing. In 1814 Charles Stewart of Shierglas rebuilt the bothy, put in a window and used it as temporary accommodation and shelter when he went shooting there. Disagreement over Stewart's shooting rights arose in 1823, with Humphrey Graham, the Duke's Edinburgh lawyer, taking statements from several gamekeepers, who knew the area well.

Lauchlan Mackintosh, aged ninety, maintained that as far back as he could remember, there were eight bothies inhabited in the summer by people tending their livestock on the shieling. He thought that at the time the 4th Duke was raising the Atholl Highlanders in 1777, Shierglas came now and then to shoot grouse when his cattle were on the shieling. In fact deer sometimes came down to pasture while the cattle were still there. He well remembered that seventy years earlier (c 1750) he helped John Crerar's father, Sandy, the Dukes' fowler, to shoot across the area and assisted him with nets for trapping birds, sometimes for three days at a time.

John Crerar remembered that tenants left the shieling every year at Lammas (early August) with their cattle and the Duke's gamekeepers impounded any they found after that date, thus freeing the pasture for deer. The pound was

Ruins of the Kirrachan Shieling where there was a small shooting bothy in 1814.

The old settlement of Clunes, above the present lodge. Cattle straying on the Kirrachan Shieling after Lammas (August) were impounded by the Clunes keeper and held here.

located near the old settlement of Clunes, situated north of the present lodge, and he remembered that the Duke was in the habit of shooting over the Kirrachan without challenge.

George Ritchie had been in the Duke's service as a gamekeeper for forty years and shot grouse across the shieling every year. He thought that no one else apart from the Duke shot there and remembered that in 1777 he pitched a tent in the shieling and shot grouse there for several days. Occasionally he remembered that a young relative "might go out for a frolic, but rarely in the season and with intervals of years".

In 1826 the case was finally settled in favour of the Duke and the following year he bought back the Shierglas feu for half the shieling. Three years later he acquired the other half for £900.[3]

Poaching

Poaching was as rampant here as elsewhere but the Clunes keepers seemed to have had more success than many in naming and sometimes even catching the offenders.

In 1813 the overseer, John Stewart, reported that his assistant, John Walker, removed a rifle from two men, Robert Robertson "in Bridgend of Strowan in the stands of Kindrochet" and Robert Gow from Calvine. He had found them with the gun in the hill above Clunes and although it was unloaded, it had obviously been fired recently.[4] Walker afterwards demanded an allowance of

whisky for travelling, similar to that given to Donald MacIntyre at Forest Lodge, otherwise "he is not able to travel the hills".[5]

Two years later, Charles Fraser from Strowan Lodge reported that he had caught Alex Macpherson in the hill above Woodsheal, on the south side of the Garry. Macpherson denied having shot anything but was suspected of having been after black game which were numerous in that part. Macpherson was a sub-tenant of John Robertson of Bohespic and had already been evicted from a farm on Invervack.[6] On another occasion, Alex Robertson, a mason, also from Invervack, was found with a pointer dog and carrying a single-barrelled shotgun which was confiscated.[7]

Clunes Lodge

Clunes Lodge 781 671 was built in 1867 and before that time tenants of the Clunes forest stayed at the Bruar Inn a few miles down the road. The lodge was extended the following year, while extensive rebuilding and enlarging took place in 1892 at a cost of £800. At the outbreak of the Second World War the lodge was turned over for the use of evacuees but by December the authorities notified the factor that Clunes had been vacated and the inhabitants transferred to Blair Castle.[8]

A track runs up the centre of the deer forest, passing two shielings, **Ruidh Dubh** (black

The Chrombaidh Bothy, 4 miles north of Clunes, with Sron a' Chleirich, on the Clunes march, in the background.

shieling) 797 697 and a mile further on, **Ruidh Ban** (white shieling) 797 709. After four miles it comes to the **Chrombaidh Bothy** 800 726. This is a substantial slated stone building of two rooms, with a two-stall stable attached. It was probably once a shepherd's house but is now used as a shelter by shooting parties and hill ponies.

John Dow was the Clunes keeper in 1884/85 and in these twelve months the following were shot: grouse 70 brace; black game 39; partridge 20; woodcock 1; snipe 11; wild fowl 1; plover 5; brown hare 3; white hare 68; rabbit 79; fox 9; weasel 13; hoodie crow 2; hawk 10; raven 2; magpie 2; jay 1 and cat 7.[9]

The forest was divided between the Kirrachan Shieling at 2,500 acres and the Clunes beat at just over 7,000 acres. In addition, ground south of the Garry of about 900 acres was included. In this area there were formerly two large settlements, now both deserted. **Woodsheal** 775 668 became depopulated in the middle of the nineteenth century but the remains of fourteen buildings, a corn drying kiln and several enclosures are still clearly visible. This was the home of Donald Robertson who led a battalion of the Atholl Brigade at Culloden and fought with great distinction. **Auchlany** (field of the enclosure) 773 670 lies across the boundary stream from Woodsheal that marked the march between Atholl and Robertson of Struan. Here there are several complete gable ends of houses

Gable ends of houses in Auchlany, on the south side of the Garry, which were inhabited until the 1930s.

still standing, on the edge of a wide expanse of grassland as silent reminders that this place was inhabited until the 1930s.

Auchlany

The tenant here in the 1820s was a Widow Macdonald who managed the farm with her son "an active lad". The factor commented that "She is a very respectable tenant. Their means are not great but they have worked well through a great arrears of debt." Her rent was £30 per year and payment was considerably impaired by several neighbouring uncooperative tenants. In 1822 the performance of the farm was as follows:[10]

Crops Sown	Acres	Bolls Sown	Return	Price	Amount £	s	d
Oats	4	4½	6½	14/-	4	11	0
Barley	1½	1½	4	17/-	3	8	0
Turnips	1½	lost					
Potatoes	1		20	6/-	6	0	0
Grass for hay	2½	lost/pasture			2	0	0
					£15	19	0
17 stone wool					6	0	0
Bought 3 cows, 3 stirks, 2 calves. Sold 5 for					7	0	0
Keeps 5 tups, 90 ewes and wedders, 25 lambs and hoggs. Sold 20 wedders					8	0	0
8 crock [old] ewes					1	12	0
					£38	11	0

From the above account it will be seen that her farm returns were little above the annual rent.

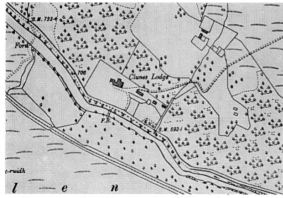

Extract from the 1900 edition of the Ordnance Survey map showing Clunes Lodge near the Garry.

KINDROCHET FOREST

The Kindrochet Forest has a common boundary with Clunes at Struan Point where 600 acres of flat moorland provided good grouse shooting. The estate was bought from the Robertsons of Kindrochet by the Duke in 1883 for £16,000 and

Colin Reid, an Atholl keeper for 31 years, has spent the last 17 of them at Clunes. (Roger Lee)

thus incorporated into the Atholl shooting grounds. Modern conifer plantations have greatly reduced the shooting, which started at Tulach Hill to the east, while the boundary dyke with Auchanruidh marked the march to the west. The central part of **Kindrochet House** 705 650, no longer a shooting lodge, dates back to 1816, probably on the site of the laird's old house. The Atholl estate added the two wings in 1886 soon after its acquisition.

James Stewart was the keeper in 1884/85 and in that year recorded the following bag: roe deer 3; grouse 356 brace; black game 55; partridge 41; woodcock 3; snipe 3; plover 11; brown hare 10; white hare 81; rabbit 25; weasel 2; hoodie crow 5 and magpie 7.[11]

Poaching Informant

The Kindrochet laird, Alastair Irvine Robertson, received a letter dated 30 April 1875 from one of his tenants, D Robertson, living in Struan, informing him of various undercover poaching activities that had taken place during his absence in Aberdeen:

I wish to tell you a thing which I have concealed till I can do so no longer. A great deal of poaching has been going on here and that for a long time and I feel compelled to tell you that the party who should prevent it are chiefly the guilty party, just William and his son. There are others at it too and it is going on still. I confess I should have told you sooner but I was afraid because William would then do me all the harm he could and did not like

Kindrochet Lodge, the oldest part being the centre section, which dates from 1816.

to inform on my neighbours. I spoke to William more than once about it and asked him to put a stop to it, knowing at the same time that he was guilty himself as well as others and he gave me little thanks for telling him. So I told him two years ago that poaching was going on at a fearful rate.

Up in the hill park, sheaves were taken out of my stooks and spread over the field for trapping and snaring and he said to me it was not his business to look after my corn. But the fault is he cannot stop the poaching when he is setting the example himself ... It was regular business every moon light night and the people on the other side of the river were laughing and making jokes about it, saying we had plenty of liberty on this side. It went such a length one night that our Minister who is lodging with us came down stairs and asked me if I was honest when I was allowing such a thing to go on behind my laird's back. I did not tell him who it was but the next night after two or three shots were fired in front of the houses he went to the door and saw Charles Robertson with his gun. He seemed to be greatly ashamed and did not say anything more. I know well enough that if William knows that I have written to you that he will do me all the harm he can, in fact he is already doing so and I dont know why, unless it be that I threatened to inform you on him. Since Miss Betsy at the Cottage died and you being so far away, there is no check upon them and they are making bad use of their liberty in many ways.

Many disgraceful things are done that you would be very angry with if you knew about them. I hope you will pardon me for writing you. My lease engagement demands me to tell you though I am very unwilling and have hesitated long to do so.

P.S. I will enclose this in the envelope marked private on the outside and I should like to see you if it suits before anything be said or done with the matter.[12]

This letter gives an example of an alleged gamekeeper-turned-poacher, usually reckoned a folk hero in that capacity and using the device of frightening someone in an effort to silence him. It was probably suspected locally, that the writer, D. Robertson was in the pocket of the laird but the outcome of the affair is not known.

Ron MacGregor for the past 3 years has been the Kindrochet keeper and before that was at Forest Lodge for 22 years.   (Roger Lee)

DALNAMEIN FOREST

The Dalnamein forest is about twelve miles long and four miles wide, marching with Clunes through Sron a' Chleirich to the east and with Dalnacardoch along its western boundary. Alex McConnachie described the ground in 1922:

> The pasture for deer is very good, with abundance of moss crop. Some of the hills are steep, but mostly smooth, with many fine corries. The forest ground is good for thirty stags, which average, clean from 13 to 14 st. The south wind suits the forest best; the worst is in the north.

> The grouse moor affords most excellent sport, particularly on the south-west side of the Garry. The bag in 1922 was over 1200 brace, but the record was made in 1897 when 1671 brace were shot. There are also black game, snipe, hares and rabbits, with a few roe. Numerous burns are available for trout-fishing and the Garry can be depended on for a few salmon.

It is difficult to explain the apparent relative absence of salmon in 1922 and a poem written about the same time seems to portray a similar sentiment:

Flow gently on sweet Garry
Doon past Dalnamein.
It frees the heart from worry,
To view the peaceful scene.

Your salmon are not many
And your trout are rarely seen.
But you please the heart of Danny
As you glide past Dalnamein.

Dalnamein Lodge

Dalnamein Lodge 752 695 lies on the north bank above the Garry but the original settlement was located in a field to the east, where the overgrown footings of at least fourteen buildings are still visible. An eighteenth century factor had little time for the tenants here, describing them as "the Dalnameiners" and the area was cleared around 1800. Plans were subsequently laid to build a large house here, which was the forerunner of the present lodge.

The Dalnamein forest was well established by the 1830s. James Thompson was the gamekeeper

Dalnamein Lodge in the early part of this century. A tennis court is to the left beside the game larder and gun room, with the keeper's cottage behind. The suspension bridge across the Garry gave access to the railway.

ATHOLL DEER FORESTS
DALNAMEIN • DALNACARDOCH • DALNASPIDAL • ERROCHTY

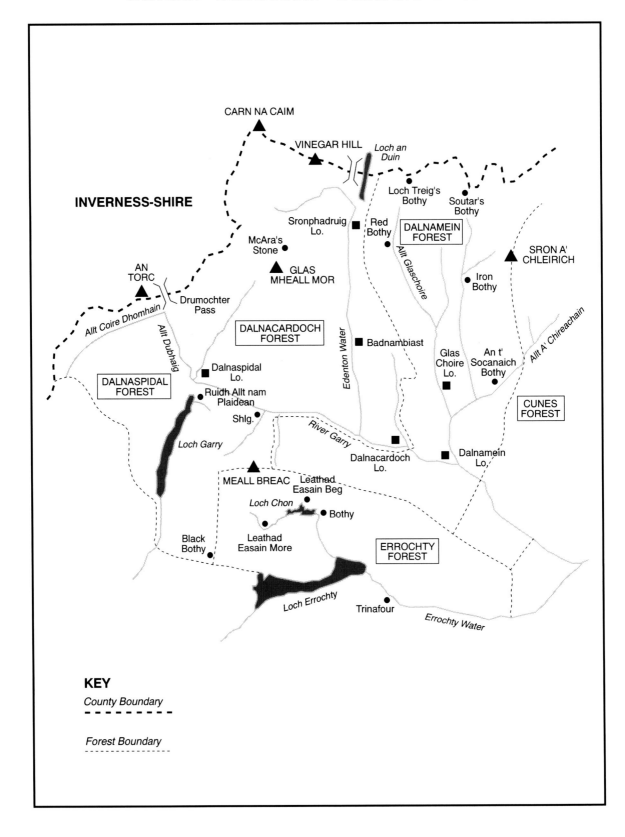

KEY

County Boundary
– – – – – – – – – –

Forest Boundary
- - - - - - - - - - - - - - - - -

"End of the Day in the Glaschoire". (Roger Lee) Left to right: George Macleod, Dalnamein keeper; the late Lord Allerton of Loddington Hall, Leicestershire; the late George Logan, under keeper; Bruce Hendry, an under keeper.

in 1884 and in that year the following bag was shot: grouse 376 brace; snipe 10; white hare 25; fox 6; hoodie crow 9 and hawk 7. The lease of the Dalnamein forest was regularly advertised and in 1928 the advertisement ran thus:

SPORTING ESTATE OF DALNAMEIN

This extends to 15,000 acres with about 1,625 acres south of the River Garry, the remainder up to the county boundary.

Dalnamein Lodge contains a small Entrance Hall, Dining Room, Large Lounge, Sitting Room, 12 principal Bedrooms, 4 Bathrooms, Butler's room, Butler's pantry, Steward's room, Store room, Servants' hall, 4 maid servants' rooms, 2 men servants' rooms, Kitchen, Housemaid's pantry, Drying room, Brushing room, Hard Tennis Court etc ...

As well as a dwelling house for the resident keeper [Keeper's Cottage], also at Riechail two miles away, there is accommodation for Gillies and a house for the shepherd, a shepherd's house on the south side of the Garry and two houses for shepherds on the side of the main road.

The number of harts to be killed annually is 30. The Grass Park at Riechail is for grazing of hill ponies.[1]

Disaster struck Dalnamein in July 1878, when it was severely damaged by fire and the ensuing repairs amounted to £1,000. Seven years later the lodge and stables were once again ravaged by fire in the spring of the year, but through great exertions on the part of the estate, rebuilding and repairs were completed for the start of the shooting season.[2]

Glas Choire Lodge

Two miles up a track to the north of Dalnamein are the remains of **Glas Choire Lodge** 753 723 often referred to as Riechael in old records. This area of about 7,000 acres was feued to Robert Stewart of Fincastle in 1669 as his summer shieling. Another one nearby is called **Allt na**

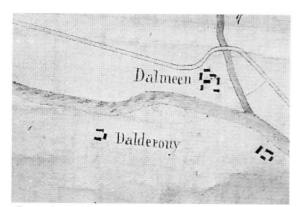

Extract from "North West Perthshire" by J. Douglas, 1821, shows the old Dalnamein settlement.

Wooden tables and benches were strategically sited for lunch breaks on the Dalnamein moor. The morning's bag of a hare and 6 brace of grouse in 1919 is displayed on the table.

Ponyman with a deer pony outside Dalnamein Lodge in 1920. The panniers usually carried an elaborate lunch which was transported to a pre-determined spot on the hill.

Sportsmen arriving at Dalnamein for the 1921 season.

A family scene on the Dalnamein tennis court in 1920.

Saobhaidh (stream of fox's den) 748 727 and was situated opposite the lodge, where there are the remains of twenty five bothies. When the tenants were removed from the shielings at the head of Glen Tilt in the 1780s to develop a deer forest, they were given this shieling for their summer grazing. The Riechael feu was given by Gilbert Stewart of Fincastle to his elder brother, Henry, in 1803 and in the 1820s he built Glas Choire Lodge. In 1827 an advertisement appeared in the *Edinburgh Courant* emphasising the advantages in leasing the lodge and its surrounding shooting:

DESIRABLE GROUSE SHOOTING QUARTERS
TO LET

The lodge of Glaschorry, with the exclusive right of shooting in the adjoining moors are to be let for this season with immediate entry. The Lodge, which is suitably furnished, affords comfortable accommodation in every respect for a sportsman. It is situated within ten miles of Blair Atholl and two miles from the Inn of Dalnacardoch. The surrounding moors which have been carefully preserved, abound with grouse and hill game. The shooting is in fact of the very highest description and will afford excellent sport during the whole season, being surrounded on all sides by the Dukes of Atholl and Gordon preserved grounds. The Inverness coach passes every day within a mile and a half of the lodge.[3]

The lodge itself contained a sitting room, and five bedrooms along with stables, kennels, a coach house, a peat-drying shed and keeper's cottage. In 1852 the feu rights were purchased by Richard Hemming for £8,000 but it was not until 1883 that the 7th Duke woke up to the fact that in law the estate still had the shooting rights over this ground. This had been specified in a clause inserted in an early feu charter "reserving all the deer that may be found at any time hereafter within the bounds of the said shealing" and had never been revoked. Believing that this meant he had full rights of deer hunting over the land in question, the Duke authorised his adjoining tenants to hunt deer in the Glas Choire. This resulted in Hemming taking out a

Bruar Lodge which lies 8 miles up the track from Calvine.

Clunes Lodge built in 1867.

Dalnamein Lodge from the south side of the Garry.

The ruins of Glas Choire Lodge, built by Henry Stewart of Fincastle in the 1820s.

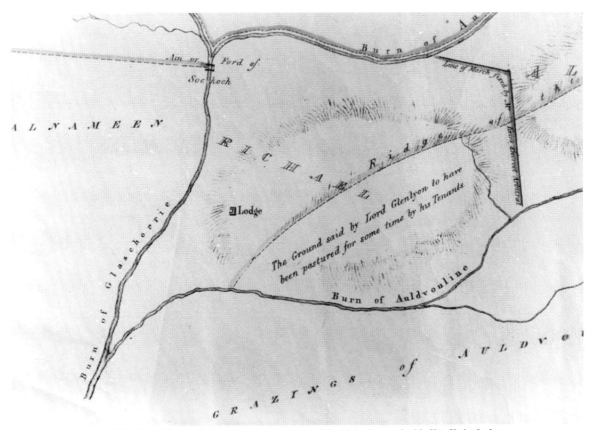

An 1843 plan of disputed ground showing the extent of the Richael ground with Glas Choire Lodge.

court action against the Duke, which was decided in the Duke's favour. On appeal, however, the decision was overturned on the unusual grounds that: "Although the deer were reserved to the Duke, he was not empowered to kill them or take them away".[4]

The Duke's reaction was to try to buy back the feu and on Hemming's death, he purchased the estate in 1892 from his daughter, Mrs Cheape for £14,250. He decided that the lodge was too small and unsuitable for improvements as it was inconveniently situated, so it was left empty. Dalnamein, however, was enlarged two years later at a cost of £1,900.

The keeper's cottage at Glas Choire Lodge was in use until the 1920s, when it was accidentally burned down by Atholl stalkers and shepherds who were waiting for the arrival of a shooting party. When they were sighted, the men departed and a spark from the embers caused the fire. Apparently the factor was successful in claiming damages from the insurance company by alleging that a tramp had gone in and lit a fire, leaving it unguarded.

Bothies

There were five bothies in the Dalnamein ground, more than in any other Atholl forest.

Loch Treig Bothy 742 800 is situated at the head of the Glas Choire, right on the county march with Inverness-shire. A herd lived here all summer and was paid £5 for a season's watching. The bothy gets its name from a Calvine man, Donald McMaster, who returned home one spring after wintering his hoggs in Morayshire and noticed a strange sheep among his flock. He put a halter on its neck and walked it all the way to Loch Treig, a distance of over fifty miles, to return it to its rightful owner. About two miles to the east and again on the county march was **Soutar's Bothy** 767 793. This was located opposite another bothy on the Badenoch side and both were known as watchers' bothies, usually manned by elderly keepers, part of whose job it was to look out for movement of deer.

The function of the Atholl watcher was not only to look out for deer but also to try to ensure that herds did not stray across the boundary into Badenoch and another laird's land. The life of a deer watcher was solitary, as he lived day and night for up to three months in the remotest part of a glen. When his bothy was in the area of an important mountain pass he frequently saw travellers, but these Dalnamein bothies were right off the beaten track and no other humans,

The Loch Treig Bothy at the head of the Glas Choire, right on the county march with Inverness.

Donald McMaster, the Calvine shepherd after whose exploit the Loch Treig Bothy was named.

apart from an occasional keeper, were seen from one week to the next.

Further down the Glas Choire is the **Red Bothy** 733 773 which used to be known as the Black Bothy until its corrugated iron roof rusted. It stands at the junction of two streams below the south-west shoulder of An Sligeanach, a 2,500 feet mountain, after which it was first named. **The Iron Bothy**, 763 762 so named because it was constructed from corrugated iron, sat at the junction of two rivers, Allt a' Mhuilinn and Allt Cragach on the site of the old shieling of Aldvoulin, where there is still evidence of twenty five shieling bothies. The Iron Bothy was still standing sixty years ago.

In his early days in Atholl, William Scrope became interested in the possibility of renting the Aldvouline shooting, said he would

The Red Bothy in the Glas Choire beside the old shieling.

Aldvouline, the shieling where the Iron Bothy was sited.

build " a good cottage on the property" and was willing to meet half the expense. He added that until it was built he would stay at the Dalnacardoch Inn but all this came to nothing when he was offered Bruar Lodge. The fifth bothy was called **An t-Socanaich** (place of the little snout) circa 773 722 and lay below the south face of Meall na Maoile, in an area now known as "the Greens", overlooking Allt a' Chireachan. No trace of this bothy or its foundations are to be found.

Dalnamein

*The stags they roam in plenty
O'er the distant hills so green,
And our host he looks for twenty
As the kill at Dalnamein.*

*With Gow and Jock and Jimmie
And a cavalcade not mean,
They sally forth to battle
From the lodge at Dalnamein.*

*When the day is wet and weary
And the stags are few and far between
We hasten back, tho' tired, still cheery,
To the smoking-room at Dalnamein.*

*But should I dare tell it,
Dan - he slips out at e'en
To try and sneak a salmon
From the pool at Dalnamein.*

*But it's wi' the Hieland Laddie
And not the grouse and green,
That he tries to fill the larder
Of hungry Dalnamein.*

The characters in the poem of 1920 were "Gow," Charles Gow the head keeper; "Jock" was Jock Campbell, handyman and gardener and "Jimmie," Jimmy Menzies, under keeper.

George MacLeod, a keeper for 40 years, of which the past 27 have been at Dalnamein. (Roger Lee)

DALNACARDOCH FOREST

Alex McConnachie described the Dalnacardoch forest in the 1920s in the following way:

> Sronphadrick is included under Dalnacardoch. Dalnacardoch was formerly a stage on the road between Dunkeld and Inverness, and its hotel is now the shooting-box of the forest ... The east watershed of the Edendon Water is the main division between Dalnacardoch and Sronphadrick and Dalnamein; on the north side is Gaick forest. The hills are grass-and heather-covered, with not much rock. All over the pasture is good, and there is much moss crop. The shelter of the corries is good and makes up for the small amount of woodland in the forest. The heaviest stag killed scaled 19st. 3 lb...
>
> The tenant is confined to a bag of forty-five stags. The average clean weight is 14½ st. About a thousand brace of grouse are killed and thirty brace of black game, besides ptarmigan and a few partridges, roe deer and rabbits, as well as wild duck. The River Garry has here too rocky a channel and too rapid a run for fishing, but an occasional salmon is caught, and trout are of course found in the burns. Goosanders and ravens breed in the forest and badgers are found in the vicinity. Foxes are few, and well looked after. The kite has been seen, but no nesting-place discovered. Snow buntings are sometimes exceedingly numerous.

Up to the middle of the nineteenth century Dalnacardoch and Dalnaspidal were combined to form the West forest of Atholl. Duncan Robertson, alias "Break" was appointed gamekeeper in 1750 and paid half a crown for every deer killed. However this was unsatisfactory as he not unsurprisingly shot any deer he found, rather than selecting good plump ones, so he was paid a flat rate of £40 Scots (£3.6.8 Sterling) a year instead and told to shoot only as and when instructed.[1]

During the time that General Wade was constructing his network of roads in the 1720s, a number of change-houses were built about every ten miles or so, where horses could be changed. Wade had his "hutt" or headquarters at **Dalnacardoch** 721 703 from where he directed the road-building in the area and this was the forerunner of the inn, strategically sited at the junction of the military road from Stirling and the Perth-Inverness highway. Charles Robertson from Blairfettie gained the contract for building "an inn and offices" at a cost not exceeding £800 Scots (£66.13.4 Sterling) and was granted a nineteen-year lease.[2]

Jock Macpherson, piper and hillman, 1856.

Aeneas Rose, piper and Master of the Dunkeld Otter Hounds, 1856.

"Murder" at Dalnacardoch

A few years after the inn opened in 1732, two soldiers from Colonel Grant's Regiment, which was stationed locally, were seen drinking in the company of Alex Stewart from Bohespic. Soon after they all left, Alex was found dead in a nearby field "with a deep wound by a sword or bayenett in his forehead". Next day the two soldiers, who came from Strathspey, were arrested, with one of them, named Grant, being locked up in Logierait jail, while the other, called Stewart, was sent to Dunkeld. Despite extensive questioning, both professed their innocence of any crime.

According to an eye-witness, the soldiers were seen leaving the inn with Stewart just before sunset. At the Trinafour road junction, Stewart was observed running for his life, with Grant in hot pursuit, throwing stones. Stewart then climbed a dyke, stumbled and fell, immediately followed by Grant who was seen standing over him. The two soldiers were next seen setting off towards Dalnamein and "after they had gone about a bow shott" returned to the place where Stewart had fallen and after a few minutes went off again. Half an hour later the body was found, which, upon examination proved that the forehead wound was very slight and that Stewart had died from a broken neck.

The officer and sergeant who were stationed at Logierait were greatly angered at not being present at the interrogation of the two soldiers. There was no love lost between the local inhabitants and the troops billeted in the neighbourhood and there were complaints that the soldiers "are allowed to stragle through the country in arms, doing no good". and it was feared that the officer would do his utmost to free the accused. There was little the local people could do in such circumstances, because, as the report to the Duke concluded, "Your Grace knows your Country is naked of arms, and no wayes able to make resistance".[3]

Dalnacardoch Inn

After the 1745 uprising the inn was commandeered as a "Barrack Hutt" where soldiers were billeted. John Macpherson, the proprietor, arranged for repairs amounting to £11.10.3 and this sum was arrived at as follows:[4]

An Account lead [laid] out on the biggings [buildings] of Dalnacardoch by John McPherson, Tacksman 1750 and 1751.

	£	s	d
To William Miller, mason, per his receipt	3	4	3
To wright and mason for the kitchen per the receipt	1	4	6
To 23½ bolls of slime att a merk each boll & 8d of carriage	2	2	6
To couples and pans bought		14	0
To ye shouldiers [soldiers] for days working at 6d per man		8	0
To the Countrymen and my manservants for wirking		4	6
To 18 horses bringing sand to the main house & ... from Bohaly		9	0
To 6 men working the above horses		3	0
To one man casting fealls [turfs] for the kitchen			6
To 2 horses & 1 man leading them home		1	6
To 2 men pouting [putting] them on		1	0
To 4 men casting the divots [sods]		2	0
To 8 horses & 4 men leading them home		6	0
To 3 men, 3 days & 3 hrs of another day pouting them on		5	0
To 4 men, 3 days powlling [pulling] heather for the stable		6	0

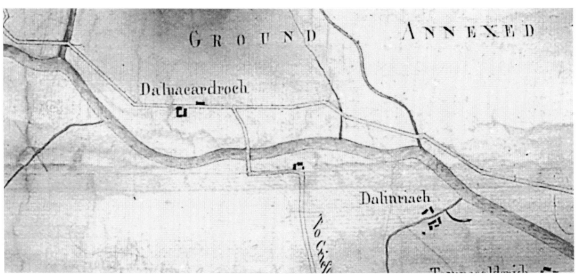

Extract from "North West Perthshire" by J. Douglas, 1821, showing the Dalnacardoch Inn and farm.

		£	s	d
To 4 horses & 2 men, 2 days bringing it home			6	0
To 3 men, 4 days puting it on			6	0
To double pleanissing nails for ye skafals & laying on the riging stones			1	0
To 5 horses & 2 men bringing ye riging stones from Tilt			3	6
The total		10	8	3
To 40 foot of Rigging Stones & Carriage from Cargill to the Bridge of Tilt		1	2	0
		£11	10	3

Mr James Small, the government factor of the forfeited estates of Struan and Lochgarry, stayed at the inn in May 1761, when his expenses amounted to £2.0.10 Sterling, made up thus:[5]

Account to Mr Small at Dalnacardoch.

	£	s	d
To Braikfast		2	6
To as hear [here] of yesterdays bill	1	1	8
To as hear of last night		3	6
To the first night		3	6
To 4 botlis ale			6
To a drame			4
To whiskies long		1	0
To the litster [dyer] from Cluny			4½
To 4 horses hay 2 nights		4	0
To Corn		2	0
To a dram & a botl ale			5½
	1	17	10
To one horse Corn & hay		1	0
	1	18	10
Yesterdays breakfast		2	0
	£2	0	10

Recd. ye above from Mr James Small factor on Strowan & Lochgarry Estate by me John McPherson. Dalnacardoch 5 May 1761.

Macpherson was still dissatisfied with the condition of the inn and farm at Dalnacardoch for which he paid an annual rent of 300 merks Scots (£16.13.4 Sterling). He was appalled to hear, that on account of all the repairs necessary, his rent was to be increased and he petitioned the factor accordingly on 16 February 1763:

> This ffarm is in a very Mountainous and stormy part of the Highlands of Scotland, at a great distance from all kinds of Provisions and fforage, and generally the winter storms are so severe that for several years past the House required to be repaired every summer.

He appreciated that it was reasonable to increase the rent to cover repairs but felt that his

A 19th century view of the Dalnacardoch Inn showing the central block built in 1774, with the stone plaque beside the entrance porch.

A 1930 view of Dalnacardoch Lodge beside the old A9, formerly the Wade road from Perth to Inverness.

were special circumstances because the severity of the weather necessitated maintenance work every summer and observed that as the inn was "at a great distance from all conveniences", he was obliged to travel 30 miles to Badenoch to collect hay and straw and all his supplies came from Perth, a distance of over 40 miles. The cost of this transport considerably reduced his profits as the animal feed he obtained was kept for his customers, while "some of his own cattle have died for want of provender".[6]

The factor was not impressed by this plea, maintaining that " this is a stage no traveller on that Road can avoid and travellers do expect not only to be well used, but to have things in a rather better and neater way on His Majesty's grounds than elsewhere".[7]

He was perhaps somewhat fed up with Macpherson and his complaining and maybe sought a way out, as he concluded in his report that "the ffactor cannot help observing that the Petitioner is not the proper landlord for Dalnacardoch as both he and his wife have been bred within the country ways..."[8]

Word of the impending removal of the tenant soon leaked out and Donald Macdonald wrote to the factor in the belief that Macpherson was to be "removed on account of bad entertainment to passengers and neglect of his business..." He put himself forward as a suitable applicant, claiming that he "is a young man fit for executing any part of the business himself and is married to a young woman educated in the Low Country..."[9] An "Execution of Removal" was raised against John

Macpherson on 19 May 1764, with the warning that he was "to flitt against the term of Whitsunday next" and ordered to pay £20 to cover damages, expenses and in case he refused to depart.

Donald Macdonald was successful in his bid to become the new tenant and in July 1765 asked for £50 to enable him "to enclose and subdivide his farm so as he might thereby be enabled to sow grass seeds in order to have good hay for horses as no good hay can be purchased within 20 miles of his farm".[10]

He was offered £25 to make these improvements, along with a loan of £50 at 5% interest. Reporting on the alterations to the inn in 1767, the factor observed that "the house is far from being so commodious as aught to be expected of a house belonging to the publick..."[11]

Donald Macdonald died in 1769 and immediately James Robertson applied for the tenancy but he was very critical of the condition of the inn and also the problems caused by its situation:

That this House is situated where both the Roads from Stirling and Perth to Inverness, Fort Augustus and other northern parts do meet, and at the foot of the high hill called Drimaugher, between the Countries of Athole and Badenough, of upwards of Thirteen computed long Miles, without so much as one Inhabitant, or house or hold to shelter or refresh in; nor can this Road be avoided by Travellers going by the highlands to the above Northern parts, which make it absolutely necessary for those coming to the said house, when towards the Evening, tho' not quite dark, to remain there till the next day, whatever their

Accommodation be. That Dunkeld which is Thirty miles distant from it to the South, and Ruthven of Badenough, of the same distance to the North, are the nearest Market places, and these not the best, which would require the greater application, diligence and address to purchase necessary provisions at so great distances ...[12]

James Robertson was highly critical of the way Macdonald had run the inn but this was rebutted by James Small who emphasised the amount of repairs he had made, adding that "he had built a kitchen and 2 rooms for his family. He has had Macdonald recommended to him by all the travellers that he [Small] had access to see." In any case, all Robertson's criticisms were to no avail as Macdonald's widow, Janet Fraser, announced her intention of staying on to run the inn, unless the forfeited estate paid her "a reasonable allowance for her outlays" which came to between £140 and £150, to enable her to leave. She maintained that her late husband had put the place in order "to render the place as commodious otherways as he could for the reception of Travellers and had the good fortune during his life to satisfy all the people of Rank and ffashion that travelled that way, that any inconveniences thay met with at this stage was to no fault or neglect of his".[13]

Since his death she had tried to follow his example and had built extensive enclosures to enable her to provide hay for horses. Further, she insisted that her husband had built "a commodious kitchen, a household family room, a Brewhouse and necessary house, [lavatory] all at their own expence". She also demanded a 41-year lease, and went on to report that she had spent £60 on building dykes and concluded by condemning the state of the inn, insisting that a new one be built in its place:

> ... The house of Dalnacardoch was originally but ill built and covered with flag slates which never could be kept water tight. From these causes it is found that the present house will not repair and as the Petitioner pays 200 merks Scots of yearly rent for the shell of the house, she is persuaded the Board will think it incumbent upon themselves to build a new house, fit for the Stage and adequate to that rent.[14]

By February 1772 there was unanimous agreement amongst the Board of Commissioners that she should be given every encouragement to stay, but not given a lease, nor allowances for repairs as these would be obtained from the next tenant.[15] The factor had received a number of signatures from people endorsing the standing and character of Janet Fraser, claiming that "We who have occasions frequently to travel The Highland Road take the liberty to recommend to the Commissioners of Annexed Estates Mrs McDonald present possessor of Dalnacardoch as a person who in her station merits the countenance and support of the Board".[16]

Thanks to Janet Fraser's persistence, a new inn was built in 1774 to a budget of £500 Sterling, which excluded carriage of materials. On its completion, a stone plaque was inserted in the wall at the front door, with the inscription "Rest a little while 1774" in Latin, English and Gaelic. Further building work took place the following year as it was felt there was "no place as a barrack for Common Travellers, soldiers ..." and to remedy this it was decided that " in place of a single room in the north wing lathed and plaistered above, he shall floor above said room, put a stair up from it to a garret ... and also lath and plaister the garret above and put in two Sky lights which will contain 12 beds".[17]

This proposal was accepted, with the factor observing that " As the main body of the New House is now ready for going into, we should make a kitchen of one of the new Parlours left rough for that purpose till the new kitchen is ready".[18]

McAra's Stone and Bothy 683 773 named after one of the famous McAra gamekeeper family. It is located on a ridge at over 2,800 feet, on the north face of Glas Mheall Mor. (Jane Fernie)

Attention then turned to the condition of the outhouses and Sir Adolphus Oughton was asked to report on their condition, which he gave in February 1776:

> 1. The Porches or Porticoes appear to be a very necessary improvement ... when built they may be covered with clapboards and pitched paper for lightness and cheapness.
>
> 2. The Harling absolutely necessary and should be done as soon as the Season permits.
>
> 3. A Stove to be got for the Great Room, as was originally intended, and plain Bars set in Brick for every Chimney to preserve the Same and make the Peat burn clear without smoking. A Carron Oven was likewise promised and cannot be dispensed with.
>
> 4. As Neatness and Cleanliness is much to be wished for, the Papering the principal Rooms will undoubtedly contribute to that end.
>
> 5. As there is no possibility of doeing without Stables it will be a saving of Expence to build the other offices at the same time. The Stables should be built on one side the Back Court, the Brew House on the other, both covered with Slates.

Stalls or travesses for six horses will be sufficient. The Shed for Carriages and Necesssary House to be built in the rear of the Back Court and covered with Clap Boards and Pitched Paper.

Sir Adolphus will endeavour to get the Back Court leveled by the Troops if any are employed on that Road this Summer: but the present situation of affairs renders that precarious.[19]

Many of Sir Adolphus's recommendations were accepted barring items one and four, which were rejected because of scarcity of funds.

Estimates were obtained for building a barn, byre and coach house and the cost of 27,000 slates was £225 Sterling, with an extra £40 for carriage from the Newtyle Quarry near Dunkeld. In 1778 an inventory of furniture in the inn revealed the following:

> In the third story six bedsteads.
> In the first flatt three bedsteads and one Carron Stove.
> In the publick room ten bedsteads, one table, two fforms and one Carron Stove.
> In the kitchen two bedsteads and a dresser.[20]

Robert Smythe of Methven Castle was the new tenant of the forest in 1821 and submitted plans for improving the sleeping quarters in the inn. He thought the dressing room was too small and having an entrance through the bedroom would be inconvenient. He offered to pay for all the alterations if the Duke would reduce his rent to £50 a year for the duration of his six-year lease but the Duke would not accept this. Later that year Smythe drew up a plan for a new dog kennel he wished to build at Dalnacardoch "with a court of wood slabs put to it 15 x 20 feet, the kennel built of stone and lime 20 x 10 feet and 5½ feet in the walls. Slated and Rygin stone roof which will cover a space of ground of 20 x 25 feet. Proposed to be built behind the byres on the north of the stable court".[21]

On 15 August 1798, Thomas Erskine from Alva, Thomas Millar and Robert Stein were staying at the inn, when they were asked one evening to give up the dining room to a shooting party from Blair Atholl. Feeling reluctant to do so, they addressed a note to "the gentlemen in the shooting party from Blair House" expressing their displeasure.[22]

What the three men did not realise until later was that the Duke was at the head of the party and "all the blame for the inconvenience and impertinence is laid upon the landlord" for not informing them of the situation. The Duke took exception to the tone of the letter so the men replied to set out their side of the case:

> It was from an ignorance that Your Grace would not have been of the party that we left the note addressed in the manner to which we understand you objected - and it is only your presence which for a moment could induce us to delay the steps which we had determined and of necessity obliged us to act under such disagreeable circumstances.

We have therefore the honour of addressing to Your Grace the substance of our former complaint. ... Had the landlord informed us of the circumstances mentioned in your note it would have avoided the trouble which his stupidity has occasioned us all ... We therefore accept Your Grace's explanation ...[23]

Badnambiast

An important old route goes due north from Dalnacardoch, following the east bank of the Edendon Water, to pass Loch an Duin on the watershed, then through Gaick and on to Speyside, considerably reducing the distance of travelling round by Drumochter. Just over two miles up this track there is a solitary building called **Badnambiast** (beast's thicket) 713 738 which is a well-built cottage now used as a barn for storing hay. It was built in the early part of the nineteenth century by James Mackenzie Stewart of Urrard who informed the Duke of his intention "to build a neat small house on it and let it out as a Shooting Quarter which I hope Your Lordship will have no objection".[24]

The cottage at Badnambiast, built in 1802 as a small shooting lodge.

Badnambiast was first feued to John Stewart of Urrard in 1737 for £33 Sterling duty a year in exchange for the land of Orchil near Aldclune. It remained in Urrard hands until 1883 when Mrs Frances (Fanny) Louisa Boxer Alston Stewart sold the feu to James Beech of the 2nd Life Guards for £13,000, a figure that surprised many, as the upset price was £4,000 less. Additional charges included feu duty at £3.6.8 and a share of the minister's stipend of £4.0.3. It was stipulated that the new owner had to graze two cows and three ponies belonging to the Superior without charge and he was not permitted to pasture his livestock on the haughland above and below the lodge.

Three years later the Atholl estate bought back the feu for £12,000. The land in this exchange covered both sides of the Edendon Water from half a mile south of Sronphadruig Lodge to the Dalnacardoch grazing which was marked by a dyke built in 1870.

A prominent cairn in memory of a shepherd, near the track at Badnambiast.

Sronphadruig

After five miles the track reaches **Sronphadruig Lodge** (Patrick's nose) 716 783 set in a secluded place amidst mature larch trees and half a mile south of Loch an Duin. The shooting beat extended to about 5,000 acres of hill and moorland, with the game consisting of grouse, ptarmigan and hares. In 1738 the ground was feued to John Stewart of Bonskeid and it was not until 1875 that the Atholl estate bought it back for £10,200, a figure which included the lodge and its furniture. Two years later additions were made to the lodge and the

"carriage road" from Dalnacardoch was completed at a cost of £750.

About 1770 the 3rd Duke pitched camp near the lodge and three tents were erected for the entertainment of his friends, with several cooks from Blair Castle in attendance. This was part of that Duke's plan to maintain control of his forests in this part of Atholl and by making a base here, he was in reach of the Glas Choire, Kirrachan and Badnambiast shooting grounds.[25]

It was only from 1820 onwards that the Stewarts were allowed to shoot here and the lodge must date from soon after this. It contains two public rooms, a small smoking room, four bedrooms, three servants' rooms, kitchen and servants' hall.[26] Adjacent was a coach-house-cum-stable and kennel with bothy attached. In the lease of 1879 tenants were permitted to shoot deer and fish on Loch an Duin for an annual rent of £300 and were also responsible for paying the gamekeeper's wages of £37 a year.

The keeper in 1884/85 was Hugh Macdonald and the bag that season included: hind 3; grouse 220 brace; ptarmigan 10; wild fowl 1; plover 2; white hare 9; fox 5; weasel 1 and hawk 2. This compares with the Dalnacardoch bag for the same season, where John McLachlan was the keeper: grouse 1,000 brace; black game 14; ptarmigan 4; snipe 7; plover 2; white hare 35; rabbit 2; weasel 7; hoodie crow 9; hawk 1; raven 4; magpie 2 and cat 3.[27]

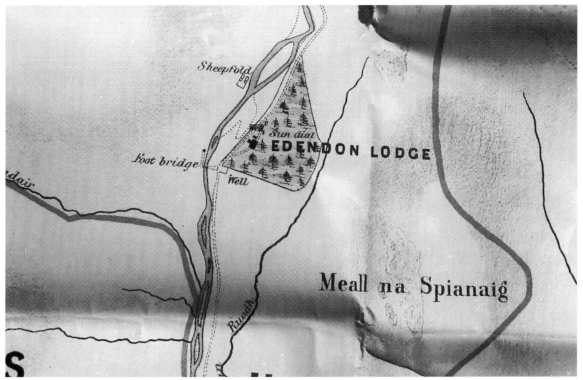

Extract from a plan of the "Glen Edendon Estate" of 1874. The lodge was first named after the river which flows through the estate but was changed to Sronphadruig after its purchase by the Atholl estate in 1875.

Sronphadruig Lodge in Victorian times. The building on the right has now gone and the lodge itself has been unoccupied for years.

It was only after Atholl had bought back Sronphadruig in 1875 and Badnambiast in 1886 that the Dalnacardoch forest was established in its own right, free from any encumbrance. It was no longer linked with Dalnaspidal and since the inn had closed twenty years earlier through the coming of the railway in 1863, it now had the use of it and Sronphadruig as its own lodges to provide easy access to the moors.

Two keepers sit outside the porch at Sronphadruig Lodge in the nineteenth century.

Sale particulars for both Dalnacardoch and Dalnaspidal were drawn up in 1942 and Major Richard Pilkington of the 9th Lancers, from Ashbourne in Warwickshire, first inspected Dalnacardoch Lodge with its 18,000 acres of deer forest in May 1943. The Atholl estate had valued Dalnacardoch at £17,500 and considered Major Pilkington's initial offer of £14,000 much below its market value. After the offer was increased to £15,000 a problem arose. The Ministry of Supply had requisitioned a large wood on the estate for timber necessary for the war effort, to save on import and shipping costs, so the Major's offer for the estate of £13,000, without the wood, was accepted.[28]

Nowadays, except in the shooting season, all is quiet at Dalnacardoch, with only the keeper, Ben Fernie and his family in residence in the keeper's cottage, as both the lodges of Dalnacardoch and Sronphadruig are internally in advanced stages of decay and unfit for human habitation.

Ben Fernie has been a keeper for 32 years, the last 22 of them at Dalnacardoch.

DALNASPIDAL AND ERROCHTY FORESTS

The Dalnaspidal forest marches with Inverness-shire to the north-west and has the railway as its northern boundary with Dalnacardoch. To the south it includes Loch Garry and four miles of moorland south of the railway, covering some 13,000 acres which include a number of corries. Alex McConnachie described the ground in the 1920s as being:

> ... good for from 800 to 1,000 brace of grouse (3,000 brace were shot in 1872!) as well as ptarmigan, wild duck, snipe and hares ... The hills are steep and grassy, affording very good pasture and moss crop in its season.

Coire Dhomhain

Coire Dhomhain (dark corrie) 631 753 was considered the best for stalking. This corrie which stretches for nearly five miles from Drumochter to the west, was known locally as "the long corrie" and was much coveted for its grazing qualities. Indeed there were times two hundred years ago when as many as a thousand oxen could be seen on the pasture.

During a court case about the march between Badenoch and Atholl in 1767, Duncan Robertson from Tulloch (in Glen Errochty) was called as a witness. At the time he was in his fifties and could remember, as a boy in the 1720s, when Lord George Murray, brother of the 2nd Duke of Atholl, arranged to have a deer hunt in Coire Dhomhain with several of his friends. A number of men, led by two gamekeepers, Alex Stewart of Innerslanie and Patrick Robertson of Blairfettie, were sent to the top of Beinn Udlamain at the west end, to drive deer down the corrie to where Lord George and his friends were waiting on top of a black knoll on the north side. Only two deer were killed in the hollow below the knoll, which became known as **Tom Mhorair** (lord's knoll).[1]

In 1827 there were thoughts of turning Coire Dhomhain into an exclusive deer forest. The Dalnacardoch gamekeeper, D.Stewart, said at the time that he would do all he could to meet the requirements of the two estates but voiced his reservations:

> Unless a continuous watch were kept, the sheep from Badenoch would get into the corrie and the herds' dogs sent after them would cross over to the south side, ranging across the whole corrie. On the south side next to Loch Garry the short distance between the south ridge of Coire Dhomain was such that his own sheep might trespass and be followed by his dogs in pursuit of them, so that he would have to employ extra shepherds to control the flock. The corrie is so narrow that it is a far quieter shelter for deer when his sheep are allowed to graze there than if preserved for deer only.[2]

Farming

An advertisement appeared in the newspapers in 1784, claiming that the Dalnaspidal ground "was extremely fit for grazing of sheep", a method of husbandry that had not yet been tried in these parts. James Welch, a large sheep farmer from Roxburgh in the Borders, took up the offer and was given a nineteen-year lease for a rent of £100 a year. According to reports, "he managed his farm in a most extraordinary manner, ploughing barren hills and endeavouring to make corn grow where it had never grown before".[3] The elements and acidic soil were against him and eventually he abandoned his grandiose plans.

There were several other attempts at farming in this area. **Allt Dubhaig** (stream of the dark pool) 646 737 joins the Garry just below the lodge and in 1812, John Campbell from Rannoch farmed the land to the west of the river, while Donald Stewart from Dalnacardoch farmed to the east. John Campbell worked away for twenty five years, with his farm consisting of a fank, wool barn and shepherd's house and his pasture land on the lower slopes of the hillside. There is no trace nowadays of the endeavours of these two men trying to eke out what must have been a precarious living in this remote place, where all is now marshy bog subjected to repeated flooding in winter.

Shielings

Throughout the eighteenth century this was a thriving shieling area, especially in Coire

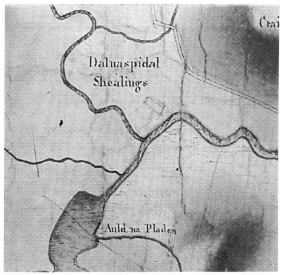

Extract from "North West Perthshire" by J. Douglas, 1821, showing the Dalnaspidal Shieling beside the military road.

Shieling at Allt nam Plaidean on the east side of Loch Garry.

Dhomhain, where there were several. Both Badenoch and Atholl livestock grazed indiscriminately and the shieling of Clashdurchoin, lying south of Allt Coire Dhomhain was a large area of rough pasture where the Dalnacardoch tenants pastured their cattle. Patrick McGuire herded 1,000 cattle here and always brought them down to the shieling pasture at night, fearing they might be stolen. Several more shielings were located beside Loch Garry and one of these was called **Allt nam Plaidean** (stream of the plaids) 644 721. Fabric was woven here on a type of primitive hand loom, where the shuttle had to be passed from side to side of the web by hand, so that only a narrow width of cloth of about 27 inches was woven. These were not "tartan" plaids but a type of coarse flannel or blanket.

General Wade's military road from Perth to Inverness was completed in 1728 and it passed close to **Dalnaspidal** (haugh of the hospice) 645 729. At that time it was only a shieling, and the remains of the bothies are still visible a hundred yards east of the present lodge. Within ten years of the building of the road, a house with byre and stable had been built and fields enclosed for cultivation.

The '45

During the uneasy and unsettled political times leading up to 1745, government troops were stationed throughout Highland Perthshire, ostensibly to maintain law and order, as is shown in a letter by the Atholl factor, Commissary Bissett, writing from his home at Kincraigie near Dunkeld on 20 July 1742:

> General Clayton hath at last ordered Semple's Regiment to take care of the country against thieving and I was at Weem yesterday with Captain Campbell, Monzie's son, concerning the proper passes where the men should be posted, such as Dalnaspidall ...[4]

The headquarters of the detachment was at Blair Atholl, where three officers, a sergeant, a corporal, two drummers and twenty one soldiers were stationed. Outstations, such as Dalnacardoch and Dalnaspidal had one officer and six soldiers. All this activity was really a smokescreen for monitoring the potential movement of pro-Jacobite followers. About a month before the Battle of Culloden, there were very few Jacobite troops in Atholl, except for Drumochter, where some had been stationed to guard the pass. Writing about this on 9 March 1746, the Duke observed:

> ... this part of the Country is now intirely free of the Rebells; the nearest of them is at a place called Dalnaspeedil, the utmost limit of Atholl, 12 miles above Blair in the road to Inverness, and from thence to Inverness. They are in possession of the whole Country, and guard all the passes so strictly that there is no getting any intelligence about them.[5]

The house at Dalnaspidal was burnt to the ground by government troops in 1746, as they pursued the retreating Jacobite army northwards. It was not rebuilt until 1796 when Laura Henrietta, Lady Bath, built a lodge there for her husband, Sir James Pulteney and major repairs were necessary by 1813:[6]

1813	£	s	d
Nails, locks, hinges to Dalnaspidal		12	6
Sundries carriage of wood	9	12	0
Carriage of lime	8	14	0
Carriage of 3,200 slates	7	4	0
Account of Work	40	0	0
Sundries Sawing Wood	7	5	11½
Alex McLauchlan for carriage of 4,000 slates	9	0	0
William Douglas for carriage of 2,000 slates	4	10	0
John Playfair for barn	96	3	8
1814			
R McLauchlan for 9,200 slates to Dalnaspidal	12	16	0
Wm Macrae for repairs to herd's house at Dalnaspidal	1	2	5

Sir A Mackenzie was the tenant at the time of these repairs and wrote to the 4th Duke indicating that he had decided to relinquish his share of the shooting tenancy and that the two remaining partners, Colonel Paterson of Castle Huntly and Colonel Smythe wished to replace him with Lord Ruthven. This was necessary as they could not afford the cost of the repairs without a third party and they stated that: "The fact is that purchasing the furniture at Dalnaspidal and making the necessary repairs to the house, comes to more than we can afford..."[7]

In the 1820s Sir Henry Goodriche took over the lease and also the furniture which belonged to Colonel Paterson, which was valued by "Mr Ballingall in Perth, a most respectable man and amounts to £153.3.6, from which is deducted £3 as the value of a boat for which it seems there is no use".[8] The boat was for fishing on Loch Garry, where as many as 730 trout had been caught in a season, with an average weight of half a pound. Apparently a 12 pound fish was not uncommon but the record catch was a 17 pound trout.

Sir Henry's lease was on a year to year basis and when the time came to renew it a few years later, he asked for compensation because of annual and extensive muir burning, or else that something be done to prevent it. George Condie, the Duke's Perth solicitor, observed that "It is impossible to come under any obligation to prevent the tenants from burning the heather, a right exercised by them under the authority of an Act of Parliament".[9]

A report from John Stewart, the ground officer at Blair, to the factor, indicates some of the problems that existed in 1830:

> The woman in charge of Dalnaspidal is willing to continue at a moderate wage and will remove at any time by giving her a weeks notice. Her wage in former times from the gentleman who had the shooting was 10 pounds Stg., and her candles yearly. But since Mart. 1829 she is there without getting any wages. The tenant this year refused to pay her and said the Duke of Atholl was to pay her wages.

> Thomas Jack Slater required to be sent to the lodge as the rain is destroying the inside of the house.

> Donald Campbell, sheep herd at Dalnaspidal will look after the shooting grounds for four shillings a week.[10]

There are no descriptions of either the interior or the exterior of the old lodge but a short extract in a letter of James Condie (George Condie's son) informs us that "the bedrooms at Dalnaspidal are all very indifferent and two of the four are exceedingly small and uncomfortable".[11]

The old lodge stood at 1,400 feet above sea level and the severity of the weather and winter storms necessitated continual repairs to all the buildings there. An indication of the severity of the weather is contained in a letter the factor wrote to the 4th Duke on 27 November 1826:

> The communication with Blair and other parts of the Highlands has been lately a good deal interrupted by the snow storm ... By Midnight the snow came on, and the wind increased to a hurricane, blowing the snow clear of the high grounds into the hollows, and carrying numbers of sheep into the burns, the snow drifts in some parts of Glen Tilt reaching to 25 feet in depth ... Owing to the very fine weather preceding Friday, none thought of securing their stock from such a sudden change. Stewart at Dalnacardoch had his sheep at Dalnaspidal, where with the exception of about 20 seen on Monday morning, they were all covered. Three of the Inverness coaches are snowed up on the road - one at the County March, where the top of the coach only is visible; another near Dalwhinnie and another farther north. Several lives have been lost. One of Stewart's herds is missing.[12]

Queen Victoria

Queen Victoria passed this way in 1861, on what was her last "Great Expedition" with Prince Albert. She was on her way back to Balmoral from Dalwhinnie, with a short stop at Blair Castle and her diary records the scene as she crossed over Drumochter:

> ... Again a little further on, we came to Loch Garry, which is very beautiful - but the mist covered the farthest hills, and the extreme distance was clouded. There is a small shooting lodge or farm, charmingly situated, looking up the glen on both sides, and with the loch in front: We did not hear to whom it belonged. We passed many drovers, without their herds and flocks, returning, Grant [Balmoral ghillie] told us, from Falkirk.[13]

Lodge Rebuilt

In the 1890s the lodge was completely rebuilt and enlarged to its present form. There were problems, however, of enlarging the part of the building which had been erected by the tenant in 1838, as the surveyor's report showed that the walls of the old building, made from rubble masonry of a very indifferent character and with little lime mortar in it, "were unable to take the additional weight of the extra floor proposed for the new lodge".[14]

Arthur Anderson of Throgmorton Street, London, a stockbroker, was the tenant at the time of the rebuilding programme and in 1892 his rent, which included staff and gamekeeper's wages, was £1,092. Part of his agreement was that the existing stable, coach house and ghillie's bothy were to be maintained in "fair repair" and the tenant, at his own expense, was to build additional stabling for four extra horses. The ghillie's bothy, known as "Peter's Bothy" after Peter MacLagan, contained two rooms to accommodate servants. At the same time, the "Iron House", made of corrugated iron, was erected with three rooms in order to house three men servants.[15] Arthur Anderson further agreed to build a billiard room as a detached part of the lodge, which remained his property when his lease expired. In a letter to the factor, dated 14 October 1892, he outlined the progress of the verandah and porch:

> I have estimated for the setting up of a porch, which will be a very handsome addition to the house and assuming everything is right, I shall have this porch constructed as soon as the snows are over next year. The old wooden porch which is showing signs of rotting will be removed.
>
> The verandah will remain a permanent structure. It will be of iron with a rolled glass roof and will have a very handsome appearance ... My desire is to have an elegant and sightly construction.[16]

When the lodge was completed it contained a billiard room ,drawing room, dining room, butler's pantry, kitchen, scullery, larder, cellar, butler's hall and a lamp room. There were fifteen bedrooms and two more for servants.[17]

In 1942 the Dalnaspidal estate was put on the market, which created some interest. In October the 13,250 acre estate was sold to Mrs Winifred Augusta Horning, wife of Lieutenant Colonel George Horning from West Grinstead in Sussex, for £10,250.[18] The present owner is a grandson of the lieutenant colonel. Considerable alterations were made to the interior of the lodge in the 1940s. Initially there had been five bedrooms downstairs but two of these were converted into a new kitchen and dining room, while a lunch room was made out of the remaining bedrooms.

The Railway

After the military road was completed in the 1720s, Dalnaspidal developed into a thriving community, which was given added impetus when the Inverness and Perth Railway Company completed the line through the Grampians in 1863 and built a station there. It contained a waiting room, while close by was the station master's house, two railway cottages, some outbuildings and a signal box. This was manned twenty fours a day by three men who lived in a

Coire Dhomhain near Drumochter, with disused railway cottages in the foreground.

A dinner plate, rimmed in blue and gold and inscribed "Dalnacardoch Hotel".

Dalnacardoch Lodge, formerly a change-house and inn on the Great North Road.

Five miles up the track from Dalnacardoch, Sronphadruig Lodge sits amongst mature larch trees.

Dalnaspidal Lodge which was completely rebuilt in the 1890s. The detached former billiard room is to the right.

railway carriage called the "dormitory", which was parked in a siding.[19] Later the "dormitory" was replaced by a row of railway cottages just over a mile down the track, at Allt Chaorach but there is no trace of them now, as they were demolished some twenty years ago to make way for the latest A9 road improvements.

Near the railway hut and close to the track is a memorial stone to "Ting" Stewart, a signalman, who, on New Year's Eve 1932 returned on a pilot engine to the station and phoned his wife from the signal box to say he was on his way home. He then set off to walk the mile down the track to his Allt Chaorach cottage but never arrived as he he was struck and killed by a train. Fellow workers erected the small stone in his memory.

The ruins of another set of railway cottages 633 757 can still be seen a few hundred yards south of Drumochter summit and near the place where Allt a' Chaorainn joins Allt Coire Dhomhain. These cottages were inhabited until the second half of the twentieth century. The nearby shieling has completely disappeared under road building operations and when the Wade road was being constructed in the 1720s a house was built here by the soldiers which John Duff from Dalnamein took over in 1730 when he pastured his cattle here for two years. At the end of that century a "large whisky house" was opened by John Stewart from Dalnacardoch. The **County March Toll Bar** 632 760 opened in 1821 and dues collected in the first year came to £177. Cockburn's Cottage was nearby, where John

The former Dalnaspidal School opened in 1891 for 4 to 5 hours a day, in winter only.

Macpherson, mail strapper (groom) was living in 1851, but with the coming of the railway that trade lapsed and William Ross, platelayer and Ronald MacDonald, rail surfaceman, became the new tenants.

The Dalnaspidal School opened in 1891 in a two-roomed building to the rear of the lodge. It was wood panelled, with a fireplace at one end and the stone walls were damp and bare. The rooms were dim as the only light came through small skylights. The school was opened only in the winter months for four to five hours each weekday and on Saturday mornings. It closed in 1929 when the new school opened on 10 September, on the top side of the railway line, near the level crossing and it finally closed in 1967.

John Kennedy, who was born at Dalnaspidal, began his working life there forty five years ago

A clipping scene in the Dalnaspidal fank in 1989. Up to 400 Blackface ewes are clipped every year.

John Kennedy the Dalnaspidal stalker for 45 years.

as a ghillie, then ponyman, until becoming the estate stalker. His son, Ian, acts as shepherd, in charge of 400 Blackface ewes and 3 cows. Up until the 1960s, crops were cultivated on the haugh land beside the river, when oats, turnips and potatoes were grown on eighteen acres, which are now permanent pasture.

Bothies

Part of the conditions in the 1892 lease stipulated that, "three rough wooden shelters for lunching in wet weather be erected in suitable sheltered accessible spots on the wild moor".[20] One of these was at the **Coire Leathanaidh Shieling** (corrie of the meadow) 673 715 where the remains of three bothies can still be seen above the Garry. Another hut, the Black Bothy, was built among the remains of another old shieling on the west bank of **Allt Pol Dubh Ghlas** (stream of the black/grey pool) 647 665, in the south-east corner of the estate. Here wooden vestiges of the old lunch hut still remain.

This hut was beside the eastern boundary where it marched with the Errochty forest, land once owned by the Robertsons. It was a common grazing area between Atholl and Robertson tenants and because of this the march was clearly defined by marked stones in the area where it crosses an uncompromising, featureless landscape of peat hags, coarse grass and heather. These stones are marked with "A" for Atholl on the west side and "R" for Robertson to the east.[21] The stone at the south end of the boundary is beside the remains of an old post and wire fence on Tomanour, a knoll at the end of a peat bog. According to an old map, the next stone was 1,263 yards due north, right in the middle of another bog and here the boundary follows a sluggish stream, which has not only obliterated the fence, but the stone also. The third stone is not 993 yards distant, as shown on the map, but about 550 yards away, half way up the hillside, right on the line of the fence. This error arose because the cartographer added this distance to the stone on the watershed, rather than the second stone. The boundary takes a right turn at

The Black Bothy was built as a shelter in the 1890s on the site of an old shieling. Loch Errochty is in the background.

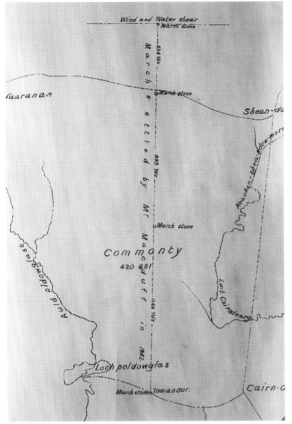

Extract from a "Plan of Auchleeks and Blairfettie" by P. McLaren, 1842, showing the boundary between Auchleeks and Dalnaspidal.

A stone on the Dalnaspidal/Auchleeks march, incised with "A" for Atholl on the west side ...

... and "R" for Robertson of Auchleeks on the east.

the watershed "where wind and weather shear," about 430 yards distant. Here, beside the corner post is the fourth stone, clearly marked with "A" and "R".

ERROCHTY FOREST

For long Glen Errochty was the heartland of Clan Donnachaidh, or the Robertsons, who by the fifteenth century, possessed most of the land in Atholl. Gradually over the centuries this possession slipped away, mostly to the Atholl family in Blair Castle, until Dundas Robertson of Auchleeks was the last remaining laird of any substance, owning most of the glen. In 1962 when he sold the estate to the Mackinlay family, this completed the eclipse of the clan as landowners in Atholl.

The forest covers an area of about 7,500 acres of land which varies in altitude from 600 feet to 2,100 feet at **Meall Breac** (speckled hill) 668 696 on the northern march. It is centred on **Loch Chon** (Loch of the Dogs) 694 679 where, at the eastern end there is a two-stall stable and bothy 694 670. Two

The Sron Chon Shieling now only becomes visible when the water level of Loch Errochty drops by about 40 feet.

Glen Errochty above Trinafour, before it was dammed and flooded in the 1950s.

Loch Chon with the two-stall stable and bothy at the east end.

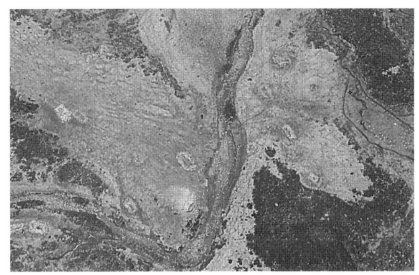

still remain visible, along a half-mile stretch of ridge overlooking the loch. **Leathad Easain More** (slope of the great waterfall) 670 673 sits astride the river from which it gets its name, as there are a series of waterfalls. Here again are the substantial remains of shieling bothies in an area which was leased three hundred years ago to Blairfettie tenants at a rental of £6 Scots and three sheep which were valued at £2 Scots each.

The 1946 game records show that in that year 20 brace of grouse, 30 stags and 50 hinds were shot during the season. The grouse bag peaked in 1953 at 336 brace and since then has declined. Errochty forest is part of the East Loch Ericht Deer Management Group and today's target is 15 stags and 50 hinds during the season.

An aerial view of footings of shieling bothies that once formed Leathad Easain More, one of the Errochty shielings.

large shielings dominate the area. **Leathad Easain Beg** (slope of the little waterfall) 690 683 lies half a mile to the north and there, the footings of ten bothies and several enclosures

CONCLUSION

As soon as John Murray succeeded to the dukedom on 5 November 1774 to become the 4th Duke of Atholl, he had a report drawn up on the condition of his estate, north of Killiecrankie. This report indicated that because it was at a higher elevation, it was more primitive in its husbandry than other parts of his estate:

> In 1774 no plan existed of this part of the Estate save and except the plan of the parks and grounds taken by Duke James around the house. No Hill grasings were let independent of Farms, except the grasing of Fealar, and the other Hill grounds were a kind of general commonty among the Tenantry - in some places even common with other Heritors. Particular spots indeed were marked out on which Sheals were built, and around these somewhat of an exclusive grasing maintained by Tenantry of Districts in the summer months. Even what was denominated Forest was studded with such Sheals, and the grasing of the deer and numbers quite reduced - scarcely more than 100 Hinds left of stock - Harts rarely in the Forest except in the Summer and rutting season, and a few in Benyglow. Implements of husbandry on [of] the worst construction. Ploughs used with four small horses abreast, a man between the centre horses walking backwards to guide the plough from stones. Scarcely a cart but with axle moving round, and with wheels solid of two pieces of wood - a load seldom exceeding 5cwt. Numbers of Sledges used with a small basket to carry coals etc. etc.

> No attempts at sown grass, Fallow, Green crop, or any kind of fit rotation. The only system, ploughing the outfield so long as it would yield even a double of the seed, then leaving it to recover, and saying it was laid down in grass. The Infield in constant tillage, mostly manured from the roofs of the Houses or the Flaughter spade - not a Farm House slated, or with any adequate offices - *with the average of nine years to run of leases.*[22]

The report highlighted that out-of-date farming methods were still being practised in this part of Atholl. The lack of properly enclosed fields in the more fertile parts meant that the continuing practice of moving domestic animals during the growing season to the shielings in the hills was to the detriment of good deer husbandry, so that by the end of the eighteenth century both hind and stag numbers were at a very low level in the old forests.

The immediate result of this was the start of implementing more modern agricultural practices, of which one factor was shutting off the high shielings in Glen Tilt for the exclusive use of deer. Although some tenants were provided with alternative summer pasture in other glens, the great exodus of people began, from farms which appeared to the estate to be too small, inefficient and uneconomic, with the result, that here, as elsewhere in Scotland, the glens were left to sheep and deer.

It is ironic two hundred years after the 4th Duke's estate report, that these glens, now devoid of people, are left as havens for wild life and hunting with an over-abundance, in some places of deer, thus giving them the apt title of "the Living Wilderness".

ACKNOWLEDGEMENTS

I am deeply grateful to a great many people in the area who have helped me in the production of this book, especially the gamekeepers, some of whom have taken me round their beats. In particular I would like to mention: Angus Cameron, Mains of Orchil; Ben Fernie, Dalnacardoch; John Kennedy Dalnaspidal; Jimmy Lean, Fealar; Gordon McGregor, Glenfernate; Ron MacGregor, Kindrochet; George Macleod, Dalnamein; Charles Pirie, Forest Lodge; Colin Reid, Clunes; Sandy Reid, Old Blair and Alister Stephen, Lude.

Landowners have not only given me access to all parts of their estates but allowed me to examine their records and I am most grateful for this. Those who have assisted me are: Roger Adams, Dalnaspidal; Major W G Gordon, Lude; David Heathcote-Amory, Glenfernate; Donald Mackinlay, Trinafour and James Teacher, Fealar. My very special thanks go to His Grace the Duke of Atholl for allowing me to research his family archives and for giving me permission to reproduce the old photographs, paintings and sketches both in Blair Castle and other properties on the estate.

Well over ninety per cent of the material in this book is from original sources, much of which has never been published before and this is the result of many hours spent researching letters, manuscripts, charters, maps and plans in the Charter Room at Blair Castle. Here, as always, the assistance of Jane Anderson, the archivist, has been invaluable in locating material and recommending possible sources. The wildlife of the glens across the centuries is covered in some detail and I must record my sincere gratitude to Roger Lee, the well-known artist from Calvine, for creating and painting the book jacket and allowing me to reproduce many of his paintings and sketches throughout the text.

It was a great personal sorrow to me that, just as this book went to print, the Duke died on 27 February 1996. Throughout our thirty-year acquaintance he always showed me much kindness and understanding. With his approval I was able to travel the length and breadth of the estate, researching and photographing and he granted me unlimited access to the whole of Blair Castle, its Charter Room and the South Wing. He took a keen interest in my research and always gave me a warm welcome when we met to discuss my latest exploits and discoveries.

I will always value our friendship and "The Living Wilderness" is published in his memory.

REFERENCES

Abbreviations

AC	Atholl Chartularies
BCCR	Blair Castle Charter Room
Chronicles	Chronicles of the Atholl and Tullibardine Families
SRO	Scottish Record Office
TGSI	Transactions of the Gaelic Society of Inverness

chapter one

Ancient Forest Laws

1. BCCR   Damages for Deer Driving litigation
2. BCCR   Forest Rights litigation
3. BCCR   Damages for Deer Driving litigation
4. Ibid
5. Ibid
6. Ibid
7. Ibid
8. Hunting and Hunting Reserves in Medieval Scotland, J. Gilbert
9. BCCR   Damages for Deer Driving litigation
10. Ibid
11. BCCR   Bundle 249
12. BCCR   Damages for Deer Driving litigation
13. BCCR   Trunk 29 I 33
14. BCCR   Bundle 247
15. BCCR   Bundle 249
16. Ibid
17. BCCR   Bundle 242
18. Nomina Shieling Place Names, J. Kerr
19. BCCR   Bundle 249
20. Hunting and Hunting Reserves in Medieval Scotland, J. Gilbert
21. BCCR   Bundle 247
22. Ibid
23. Chronicles Volume 1
24. BCCR   Trunk 45 (4) 202
25. BCCR   Trunk 45 (4) 203
26. BCCR   AC Volume 1
27. Ibid
28. Chronicles Volume II

chapter two

Atholl Deer Forests

1. BCCR   Bundle 247
2. BCCR   Bundle 839
3. Ibid
4. BCCR   Trunk 43 IV A 22
5. Ibid
6. Ibid
7. Ibid
8. BCCR   AC Volume 1
9. Ibid
10. Ibid
11. Ibid
12. Ibid
13. Ibid
14. BCCR   AC Volume 2
15. BCCR   Bundle 249

16. BCCR   Trunk 40 I B 18
17. BCCR   Trunk 54 (3) 246
18. BCCR   Trunk 68 (8) 143
19. BCCR   Trunk 68 (14) 9
20. BCCR   Trunk 68 (14) 14
21. BCCR   Trunk 68 (14) 33
22. BCCR   Trunk 68 (14) 182
23. Chronicles Volume IV
24. BCCR   Trunk 69 (2) 245
25. BCCR   Trunk 69 (2) 258
26. BCCR   Trunk 69 (2) 276
27. BCCR   Trunk 69 (2) 331
28. BCCR   Trunk 48 (5) 77
29. BCCR   Trunk 69 (2) 318
30. BCCR   Trunk 69 (3) 33
31. BCCR   Bundle 242
32. BCCR   Trunk 68 (12) 102
33. BCCR   Trunk 68 (5) 13
34. BCCR   Trunk 68 (8) 38
35. The Deer and Deer Forests of Scotland, A. McConnachie
36. BCCR   Trunk 69 (1) 50
37. BCCR   Game Books, 1884-1885
38. BCCR   Trunk 40 I B24
39. Ibid
40. The Hound and the Hawk, J. Cummins.

chapter three

Gamekeepers and Sportsmen

1. BCCR   Trunk 40 I B 17
2. Chronicles Volume IV
3. BCCR   Bundle 245
4. BCCR   Trunk 65 (11) 211
5. BCCR   Trunk 69 (5) 340
6. BCCR   Bundle 242
7. BCCR   Trunk 69 (2) 85
8. BCCR   Trunk 69 (2) 159
9. BCCR   Trunk 69 (2) 235
10. TGSI   Volume LII A MacRae
11. BCCR   Trunk 68 (14) 53
12. BCCR   Trunk 69 (3) 468
13. BCCR   Trunk 69 (4) 87
14. BCCR.   Trunk 69 (4) 155
15. BCCR   Trunk 69 (5) 130
16. BCCR   Bundle 242
17. BCCR   Forests Rights litigation
18. Days of Deer Stalking...   W. Scrope
19. Chronicles Volume IV
20. BCCR   Bundle 245
21. Chronicles Volume VI
22. BCCR   Bundle 251
23. Chronicles Volume VI
24. BCCR   Trunk 68 (14) 261
25. Random Shots, J. Irvine Robertson
26. Ibid
27. Ibid
28. BCCR   Trunk 69 (4) 108
29. BCCR   Trunk 69 (4) 232
30. BCCR   Trunk 69 (4) 345
31. Chronicles Volume IV

chapter four

Poaching and Poachers

1. BCCR   Damages for Deer Driving litigation
2. BCCR   Trunk 43 IV A 19
3. BCCR   Trunk 47 (7) 77
4. The Deer and Deer Forests of Scotland,
   A McConnachie
5. Ibid
6. BCCR   Trunk 48 (11) 10
7. BCCR   Trunk 48 (7) 4
8. BCCR   Trunk 69 (2) 144
9. BCCR   Bundle 246
10. BCCR   Trunk 69 (6) 78
11. Romance of Poaching in the Highlands,
    W. McCombie Smith
12. Ibid

chapter five

Fealar Forest

1. BCCR   Bundle 249
2. BCCR   AC Volume I
3. BCCR   Bundle 249
4. Chronicles Volume III
5. BCCR   Trunk 48 (2) 95
6. BCCR   Trunk 48 (3)66
7. BCCR   Trunk 68 (12) 85
8. BCCR   Trunk 68 (12) 317
9. BCCR   Bundle 250
10. BCCR   Trunk 69 (1) 312
11. BCCR   Trunk 69 (4) 365
12. BCCR   Trunk 69 (4) 431
13. BCCR   Bundle 1544
14. BCCR   Bundle 245
15. Ibid
16. BCCR   Bundle 250
17. BCCR   D3.91 Fealar Lodge alterations
18. Chronicles Volume VI
19. The Deer and Deer Forests of Scotland,
    A. McConnachie

chapter six

Seven Shielings and Lude Forests

1. BCCR   Seven Shielings litigation
2. Ibid
3. Ibid
4. Ibid
5. Ibid
6. Ibid
7. BCCR   Trunk 47 (14) 54
8. BCCR   Trunk 48 (3) 22
9. BCCR   Trunk 48 (3) 45
10. BCCR   Trunk 68 (3) 38
11. BCCR   Trunk 68 (2) 351
12. The Romance of Poaching in the Highlands,
    W. McCombie Smith
13. BCCR   A.1 Plan of Blair ... J. Stobie.
14. BCCR   Lude Grazing March
15. BCCR   Trunk 69 (1) 240
16. Chronicles Volume IV
17. BCCR   Game Books 1884-1885
18. BCCR   Particulars of the Barony of Lude... 1820
19. BCCR   Forest Rights litigation

chapter seven

Tarf Forest

1. Chronicles Volume I
2. BCCR   Trunk 45 IV 243
3. BCCR   Trunk 65 (2) 99
4. Monarchs of the Glen, D. Hart-Davis
5. BCCR   AC Volume 1
6. BCCR   Trunk 47 (3) 56
7. BCCR   Bundle 245
8. Ibid
9. Ibid
10. BCCR   Trunk 48 (3) 94
11. BCCR   Bundle 250

chapter eight

Tilt and Beinn a'Ghlo Forest

1. BCCR   Trunk 49 (2) 95
2. BCCR   Trunk 48 (4) 19
3. BCCR   Trunk 68 (3) 13
4. BCCR   Trunk 68 (7) 189
5. BCCR   Trunk 69 (2) 330
6. BCCR   Trunk 29 I 15
7. Chronicles Volume II
8. Ibid
9. BCCR   Trunk 48 (8) 92
10. BCCR   Trunk 49 (8) 96
11. BCCR   Trunk 54 (2) 187
12. BCCR   Trunk 68 (11) 141
13. BCCR   Trunk 68 (11) 120
14. BCCR   Trunk 68 (11) 169
15. BCCR   Bundle 1573
16. BCCR   Trunk 68 (12) 229
17. BCCR   Trunk 59 (6) 14
18. BCCR   Trunk 68 (10) 270
19. BCCR   Trunk 68 (12) 19
20. BCCR   Trunk 68 (12) 95
21. BCCR   Trunk 68 (12) 360
22. BCCR   Trunk 68 (13) 183
23. BCCR   Trunk 68 (14) 307
24. BCCR   Trunk 68 (14) 318
25. BCCR   Trunk 68 (14) 350
26. BCCR   Trunk 69 (2) 151
27. Days of Deer Stalking ... W. Scrope
28. Chronicles Volume IV
29. BCCR   Trunk 68 (2) 307
30. Chronicles Volume IV
31. BCCR   Bundle 60
32. BCCR   Trunk 69 (5) 23
33. BCCR   Trunk 69 (6) 67
34. Chronicles VolumeVI
35. BCCR   Bundle 60

chapter nine

West Hand Forest

1. BCCR   Trunk 59 (6) 14
2. BCCR   Bundle 833
3. BCCR   Trunk 68 (5) 19
4. Chronicles Volume IV
5. BCCR   Trunk 68 (3) 199
6. BCCR   Trunk 68 (14) 182
7. BCCR   Trunk 69 (6) 59
8. BCCR   Trunk 69 (6) 62
9. BCCR   Death of a Notable Atholl Highlander
10. BCCR   Trunk 58

chapter ten

Bruar Forest

1. BCCR   D2.12.28 Sketch of Cabir Bhruar
2. BCCR   Trunk 48 (11) 171
3. BCCR   Trunk 68 (13) 237
4. BCCR   Bundle 245
5. BCCR   Trunk 48 (2) 60
6. BCCR   Trunk 68 (13) 281
7. BCCR   Bundle 250
8. Ibid
9. BCCR   Trunk 68 (14) 309
10. BCCR   Bundle 245
11. BCCR   Trunk 69 (1) 263
12. BCCR   Bundle 250
13. BCCR   Trunk 69 (2) 330
14. BCCR   Trunk 69 (2) 341
15. BCCR   Trunk 69 (4) 25
16. BCCR   Trunk 69 (4) 32
17. BCCR   Bundle 246
18. BCCR   D2.2 Plan of Bruar Lodge
19. BCCR   Bundle 250
20. BCCR   Game Books 1866-1867
21. BCCR   AC Volume 1
22. BCCR   Trunk 43 IV A.20
23. BCCR   Trunk 43 IV A.31

chapter eleven

Clunes and Kindrochet Forests

1. BCCR   AC Volume 1
2. BCCR   Trunk 69 (2) 322
3. Chronicles Volume IV
4. BCCR   Trunk 68 (5) 287
5. BCCR   Trunk 68 (5) 296
6. BCCR   Trunk 69 (3) 453
7. BCCR   Trunk 69 (4) 531
8. Chronicles Volume VI
9. BCCR   Game Books 1884-1885
10. BCCR   Atholl Estate Rentals 1822
11. BCCR   Game Books 1884-1885
12. James Irvine Robertson.

chapter twelve

Dalnamein Forest

1. BCCR   Bundle 248
2. Chronicles Volume IV
3. BCCR   Bundle 839
4. Chronicles Volume IV

chapter thirteen

Dalnacardoch Forest

1. BCCR   F.519
2. Highland Highways, J. Kerr

3. Chronicles Volume II
4. SRO   E767/23/1
5. SRO   E767/24/7
6. SRO   E767/12/2
7. SRO   E767/12/2/2
8. Ibid
9. SRO   E767/12/3/1
10. SRO   E767/2/5
11. SRO   E767/34/1
12. SRO   E767/12/7/1
13. SRO   E767/34/3
14. SRO   E767/34/4
15. SRO   Ibid
16. SRO   E767/34/7/2
17. SRO   E767/34/6
18. SRO   Ibid
19. SRO   E767/34/9
20. SRO   E767/44
21. BCCR   Trunk 68 (11) 131
22. BCCR   Trunk 59 (5) 178
23. BCCR   Trunk 59 (5) 179
24. BCCR   Trunk 48 (3) 14
25. BCCR   Bundle 839
26. BCCR   Bundle 248
27. BCCR   Game Books 1884-1885
28. Chronicles Volume VI

chapter fourteen

Dalnaspidal and Errrochty Forests

1. BCCR   Bundle 250
2. BCCR   Trunk 69 (3) 135
3. BCCR   Trunk 33 XI
4. Chronicles Volume II
5. Chronicles Volume III
6. BCCR   Trunk 68 (3) 141
7. BCCR   Trunk 68 (3) 40
8. BCCR   Trunk 69 (4) 55
9. BCCR   Trunk 69 (3) 415
10. BCCR   Trunk 69 (6) 551
11. BCCR   Bundle 1301
12. Chronicles Volume IV
13. Leaves from the Journal of our Life in the Highlands, ed. A Helps.
14. BCCR   Bundle 1752
15. Ibid
16. Ibid
17. BCCR   D3.93 Plan of Dalnaspidal Lodge
18. BCCR   Atholl Properties Volume 2
19. Railway Childhood, MS Lillian King
20. BCCR   Bundle 1752
21. "Estate of Auchleeks and Blairfettie", P. McLaren
22. Chronicles Volume IV

BIBLIOGRAPHY

PRIMARY SOURCES

CHARTER ROOM, BLAIR CASTLE

Atholl Chartularies

Volume 1	1706 - 1724
Volume 2	1726 - 1739
Atholl Properties Volume 2	1932 - 1950
F. 519 Extracts from Chartularies of entries referring to Forests of Atholl	

Trunks

29	Correspondence	1579 - 1660
33	Dalnaspidal Grazings	1791 - 1793
40	Papers concerning game, fishing	1723 - 1799
43	Instructions to Foresters	1706 - 1712
45	Correspondence	1699 - 1721
46	Correspondence	1721 - 1744
47	Correspondence	1745 - 1761
48	Correspondence	1800 - 1810
49	Correspondence	1762 - 1769
54	Correspondence	1770 - 1774
58	Correspondence	1838 - 1860
59	Correspondence	1794 - 1799
65	Correspondence	1775 - 1793
68	Correspondence	1811 - 1824
69	Correspondence	1825 - 1830

Bundles

3	Donald MacBeath Correspondence 1858
60	Glencrinie Peats cast for Forest Lodge 1827
242	Statistics as to deer killed 1830 - 1914
243	Shooting rentals 1864 - 1912
245	Correspondence concerning Atholl Deer Forests 1909
	Observations upon a red deer forest (Crerar) c. 1800
	Historical details of Feith Uaine Bothy 1806 - 1909
246	Poaching correspondence 1823 - 1860
247	Rights of Atholl Forestry 1854 - 1857
248	Sporting Estates of Dalnacardoch and Dalnaspidal 1930
249	Correspondence regarding Deer Forests, Shielings and Keepers 1675 - 1829
250	Correspondence relating to Shootings, lets and poaching 1821 - 1866
251	Description of Donald MacBeath
833	Papers concerning poaching 1805 - 1830
839	Memorial and queries concerning right of killing game in Atholl 1829
1301	Correspondence regarding poaching 1850
1466	Life of John Crerar 1750 - 1840
1544	Correspondence 1857
1549	Notes about Donald Macbeath in the Crimea
1573	Description of 1822 Coronation by Lady Elizabeth Murray
1735	Leases of Kindrochet Lodge 1882 - 1936
1736	Leases of Forest Lodge 1864 - 1937
1737	Leases of Glen Bruar Lodge 1841 - 1938
1738	Leases of Dalnamein Lodge 1827 - 1939
1744	Leases of Clunes Lodge 1844 - 1948
1751	Particulars of the Deer Forest of Fealar 1882
1752	Leases of Dalnaspidal Lodge 1859 - 1938
1753	Leases of Dalnacardoch and Sronphadruig Lodges, 1837 - 1940
1754	Leases of Dalnaspidal Lodge 1862 - 1864
1866	Estate Correspondence 1921

Maps and Plans

A.1	Plan of Blair in Atholl, Forests of Tarff, Benechrombie in Perthshire James Stobie 1780
A.3	Counties of Perth and Clackmannan James Stobie 1783
A.4	North East Quarter of Perthshire James Stobie, copied by James Stirton 1815
A.5	North West Perthshire J Douglas 1821
A.10	Dalnaspidal, Dalnacardoch and Upper Glen Garry
D.2.2	Plan of Bruar Lodge 1838
D.2.12.26	Plan and Elevation of Bridge at Poll Tarff 1770
D.2.12.28	Sketch of Cabir Bhruare 1789
D.2.12.37	Ground plan of Forest Lodge 1882
D.2.32	Map of Atholl Deer Forests
D.2.35	Map of Dalnaspidal, Dalnacardoch Forests
D.2.55	Notes of Shooting Grounds to let 12 August 1825
D.3.91	Fealar Lodge, suggested alterations 1911
D.3.93	Plan of Dalnaspidal Lodge Dec. 1903
D.5.11	Sketch of Shooting Ground of Upper Glen Bruar 1833
D.5.12	Sketch of Part of the West Forest
D.5.40	Plan of disputed hill between Lord Glenlyon and Captain Beaumont 1843

Ordnance Survey 6" 1900 Edition Perthshire
Trunk 8 Parcel 4 (10) Plan of Glen Edendon 1874

Legal Papers

Action of Reduction of Contract 1716 and Decreet Arbitral 1761 relating to Seven Shielings - General Robertson v Duke of Atholl 1803

Action for Damages for Deer Driving from Common of Glen Tilt - General Robertson v Duke of Atholl 1806

Action for Damages for Muirburning on the Seven Shielings - Duke of Atholl v General Robertson 1809

Forest Rights - Duke of Atholl v James Patrick McInroy 1858 - 1862

Game Books

Atholl Deer Forests	1783 - 1824
Atholl Deer Forests	1866 - 1867
Atholl Deer Forests	1884 - 1885

PHOTOGRAPHIC SOURCES

Atholl Country Collection, Blair Atholl
Blair Castle
Clan Donnachaidh Museum, Bruar
Jane Fernie, Dalnacardoch
John Gow, Muthill
Roger Lee, Calvine
Ron MacGregor, Kindrochet
Perth Museum & Art Gallery
James Teacher, Fealar

MISCELLANEOUS

Lillian King, "Railway Childhood" (Dalnaspidal)
James Irvine Robertson, Letter to A. Irvine
Robertson regarding poaching 30 April 1875
General Register Office for Scotland, Forfeited
Estate Papers, Struan and Lochgarry:
E767; 2/5; 7/2; 12/2,5,7; 12/3 ; 12/7; 23/1; 24/7; 34/1,
3, 4, 6, 7, 9;44
Rear Admiral J D Mackenzie: Estate of Auchleeks
and Blairfettie, surveyed by P. Maclaren 1842

SECONDARY SOURCES

Atholl, 7th Duke of: Chronicles of the Atholl and
Tullibardine Families. 5 volumes 1908
Barbour, Margaret: Memoir of Mrs Stewart
Sandeman 1883

Beaumont, Richard: Purdeys the Guns and the
Family 1984
Cummins, John: The Hound and the Hawk 1988
Gaffney, Victor: Shielings of the Drumochter.
Scottish Studies Volume II 1967
Gilbert, John: Hunting and Hunting Reserves in
Medieval Scotland 1979
Hart-Davis, Duff: Monarchs of the Glen 1978
Helps, Arthur (ed): Leaves from the Journal of our
Life in the Highlands 1868
Highlander, The: 1877
Kerr, John: Atholl Shieling Names. Nomina
Volume XI, 1987; Highland Highways, 1991
Mackellar, Mary: The Shieling, its Tradition and
Songs. Transactions of the Gaelic Society of
Inverness Volume XV 1888-89
Mackintosh, Alexander: [The] Driffield Angler 1806
MacRae, Alec: A Manuscript by John Crerar.
Transactions of the Gaelic Society of Inverness
Vol LII
McCombie Smith, W: Men or Deer in the Scottish
Glens or Facts about the Deer Forests 1893. The
Romance of Poaching in the Highlands of
Scotland 1904
McConnachie, Alex. Inkson: The Deer and Deer
Forests of Scotland 1923. Deerstalking in
Scotland 1924
Pennant, Thomas: A Tour in Scotland in 1769 1774
Robertson, James: General View of the Agriculture in
the County of Perth 1799
Robertson, James Irvine (ed): Random Shots 1990
Salmond, J B: The Old Stalker 1936
Scrope, William: Days of Deer Stalking in the Forest
of Atholl 1847
Winans, Walter: The Sporting Rifle 1908

INDEX